Scot —
Thought you would be
enjoying this book to
read it _and_ to test out
its suggestions ☺ Hope
this year brings you
☮, ♡, and a new 🏠 !
Love,
Emma's Mom, Maura, whatever ☺

YINGER ...
...NTA PUMP'N ALE (ORGANIC)
EL TORO POPPY JASPER 5.37
...RESTONE OAKTOBERFEST 5...
...AGUNITAS DAYTIME 4.6...
...HENSTEPHAN FESTBIER 5...
...CKER · PSCHORR OKTOBER...
...SPRINGS ELECTION SESSION 1...
...AGASH WHITE 5% $6.50
...KEASY PIER #98 RYE 5.5%
#1
...AN · PERSEVERANCE 25TH ANNIV.
...NER FEST WIESN 6%
...RAU OKTOBERFEST 6...

OTHER BOOKS AUTHORED OR COAUTHORED BY JANET FLETCHER

Margrit Mondavi's Sketchbook,
with Margrit Biever Mondavi

*The Cakebread Cellars American Harvest
Cookbook* with Jack and Dolores Cakebread
and Brian Streeter

Kokkari: Contemporary Greek Flavors,
with Erik Cosselmon

Eating Local

My Calabria, with Rosetta Costantino

Cheese & Wine

The Niman Ranch Cookbook,
with Bill Niman

Four Seasons Pasta

Foods of the World: San Francisco

Savoring America (lead writer)

Michael Chiarello's Casual Cooking,
with Michael Chiarello

Napa Stories, with Michael Chiarello

The Cheese Course

New American Cooking: California

Cooking for Yourself

Classic Pasta at Home

Fresh from the Farmers' Market

Pasta Harvest

More Vegetables, Please

French Home Cooking, with Hallie Donnelly

Grain Gastronomy

Menus for Entertaining, with Hallie Donnelly

Cooking A to Z (contributing writer)

Italian Cooking, with Hallie Donnelly

Appetizers and Hors d'Oeuvres,
with Hallie Donnelly

Cheese & Beer

JANET FLETCHER

WITH ASSISTANCE FROM ADAM DULYE

**Andrews McMeel
Publishing, LLC**
Kansas City · Sydney · London

Andrews McMeel Publishing, LLC
an Andrews McMeel Universal company
1130 Walnut Street, Kansas City, Missouri 64106
www.andrewsmcmeel.com

13 14 15 16 17 SDB 10 9 8 7 6 5 4 3 2 1

ISBN: 978-1-4494-2184-7

Library of Congress Control Number: 2012911292

Design: Ed Anderson
Photography: Ed Anderson
Prop Stylist: Carol Hacker
Stylist Assistant/Calligrapher: Sherry Olsen

www.janetfletcher.com

Cover cheeses, left to right: Grayson, Abbaye de Belloc,
Echo Mountain Blue

Title page cheeses, left to right: Grayson, Dolcetoma,
Echo Mountain Blue

ATTENTION: SCHOOLS AND BUSINESSES
Andrews McMeel books are available at quantity
discounts with bulk purchase for educational, business,
or sales promotional use. For information, please
e-mail the Andrews McMeel Special Sales Department:
specialsales@amuniversal.com.

LAGERS

SO MANY CHOICES, SO LITTLE TIME

Nobody needs convincing that beer and cheese go together. Tangy Cheddar with an India Pale Ale (IPA). Buttery blue cheese with a malty doppelbock. Even nachos and a ballpark lager make the case. But the boom in craft beer and the blossoming interest in artisanal cheese have conspired to inundate us with choices. So many beers, so many cheeses, so little time.

If you're satisfied with a tasty beer in your glass and a favorite cheese on the table, seek no further. But your pleasure will likely spike if you put some thought into the match. When you serve a toasty Märzen that echoes the toffee aroma in aged Gouda, or find a triple-cream cheese that mellows the bitter, roasted notes of a stout, you treat yourself and your guests to an experience. You also give the craft brewer and the artisanal cheesemaker their due by putting their wares in the best possible light.

Cheese & Beer aims to boost your enjoyment of both these favorites by steering you to some proven pairings. But, more important, this volume should equip you to continue the journey on your own by familiarizing you with the major beer styles and the kinds of cheeses that complement them. With so many expertly crafted options available to fans of beer and cheese, every day brings the possibility of discovery.

In the pages to come, you will find the world's beers grouped by style to give you a framework for tasting. Once you know what to expect from amber ale or Imperial stout, you can select compatible cheeses even for brews you have never tasted. A beer's style—often stated on the label—tells you much of what you need to know: whether the beer is likely to be malty, fruity, or grippingly bitter; fiendishly high in alcohol or easy to drink; smooth as velvet or prickly with carbonation. Style is shorthand you can rely on to steer you to suitable cheeses; or, conversely, with cheese in hand, you can turn to the chart on page 94 to find beer styles that work.

But now the disclaimer. With few exceptions, beer styles don't bow to any laws. Only tradition and convention dictate the appropriate bitterness for an IPA, the typical aromas in a *saison*, or an acceptable hue for American pale ales. Organizations like the Beer Judge Certification Program and the Brewers Association issue style descriptions as a reference for brewers and competition organizers. But brewers, especially American craft brewers, delight in coloring outside the lines, devising brews that no one has ever attempted and that may not fit neatly anywhere. Attempting to corral the world's beers into categories is a crazy-making endeavor, as others who have tried it acknowledge. Just when you think you have a workable scheme, you find more beers that refuse to conform.

For competition purposes, style czars like the Brewers Association recognize dozens of distinctive niches. The more categories, the more medals. Even so, these beer-world chieftains have to revise the categories regularly to accommodate trends. New styles—such as Imperial IPAs—emerge over time, as brewers dream them up and consumers gravitate to them. Other styles fade for lack of interest or changing tastes.

Certainly the twenty-three styles showcased in this book don't tell the whole craft-beer story. But they cover a lot of ground, focusing on the most widely available styles in retail shops. Like the major branches on a tree, they provide a structure, but the side shoots flesh out the scene. In brewpubs and in well-stocked markets, you will surely discover beers in styles that aren't mentioned in these pages—rye beers, for example, or black lagers. To find good cheese matches for them, peruse this book for a beer-style sibling—a featured style with a similar mouthfeel and comparable levels of malt aroma, bitterness, and alcohol.

Exploring craft beers and the cheeses that love them is like a road trip with no destination. Consider this book your invitation to a lifelong adventure, a pastime that can add pleasure to every day. Even if you're a newcomer to craft beer or artisan cheese, you will quickly develop opinions about pairings once you start paying attention. Keep on tasting (no hardship there) and trying to put words to the aromas, textures, and flavors you note. It may be helpful to hear what more knowledgeable tasters have to say, but don't conclude that your reaction should be the same.

"Do not miss your own pairing experience trying to find someone else's," advises Adam Dulye, chef and partner at Monk's Kettle and Abbot's Cellar, popular San Francisco gastropubs. "What you taste, smell, and feel is unique to you."

MAKING MARRIAGE WORK

Beer and cheese have contributed to human contentment for millennia, but only in recent times has the average consumer had so many choices. True, America boasted more breweries in the past than it does today—an estimated thirty-two hundred in the 1870s, thanks largely to the enterprise and thirst of Dutch, German, Irish, and British immigrants. But these were primarily small ventures, serving a local clientele. Until advances in railroads, bottling, and refrigerated transport made national brands possible, people of moderate means largely drank local.

The number of American breweries declined steadily in the century following 1880. As larger, well-financed breweries began to expand nationally, local breweries couldn't compete. Many of these small breweries didn't survive Prohibition. Closures and consolidation continued, especially after World War II. By the late 1970s, America was down to 101 commercial brewers.

And then, with a vengeance, the tide turned. In 1979, President Jimmy Carter eased restrictions on home brewing, fueling a boom among do-it-yourselfers. Many of these neophyte brewers eventually opened microbreweries or brewpubs. The renaissance of craft brewing was under way. In the United States alone, the Brewers Association counted 250 new breweries in 2011, bringing the total to just under 2,000.

The same perishability issues that affected beer distribution in the past limited the offerings at American cheese counters. Hefty aged wheels like Cheddar, Gouda, Emmental, and Parmigiano Reggiano could and did cross oceans, but softer cheeses weren't up to the journey. The development of refrigerated trucking and container shipping has revolutionized the marketplace, bringing us cheeses from around the globe. And the burgeoning American artisanal cheese industry has only enhanced the bonanza. The American Cheese Society's annual professional competition has more entries every year, with almost seventeen hundred cheeses submitted for judging in 2011.

The wealth of choices can be tantalizing—or paralyzing, depending on your tolerance for risk. To make your way through the onslaught of craft beers and cheeses, you'll need a strategy—an approach to pairing that improves your outcomes and even produces some occasional epiphanies.

Let's start with this premise about cheese and beer pairing: Success largely rides on contrasts and complements. The most pleasing matches arise from juxtaposing opposites (contrast) or conjuring echoes (complement). Imagine a luscious triple-cream cheese with a highly effervescent pilsner: That's contrast at work. Or consider the overlapping aromas in a malty porter and a nutty Comté, a match that clicks because of the complementary scents. The notions of contrast and complement will guide you to the most rewarding marriages. If you consider the following attributes as you taste, you will almost instinctively find yourself gravitating toward a contrasting or complementary pairing.

TEXTURE: The tongue-tingling prickle of carbonation makes beer refreshing and recalibrates the palate after a sampling of fatty cheese. But beers range widely in their degree of carbonation, from the relatively low levels in high-alcohol beers like barley wines and Imperial stouts to the vigorous mousse in a Belgian-style strong golden ale or a pilsner. And bottled beers, especially bottle-conditioned beers (those refermented in the bottle), tend to be fizzier than the same beer on tap.

Cheese can be moist, soft, and silky, like Brie, or dry and brittle, like well-aged Gouda. It can be light on the tongue, like ricotta, or dense and fudgy. With your matchmaking, you can highlight textural similarities—pairing a velvety barley wine with creamy Cashel Blue, for example—or engineer an enjoyable contrast.

INTENSITY: In general, pair delicate cheeses with relatively light-bodied beers—fresh mozzarella with a hefeweizen, for example. Aged cheeses with complex, concentrated flavors need brews with more richness and strength. By matching intensities, you lessen the risk that either side will vanquish the other. Just as a tennis match is more riveting when the players are of comparable caliber, beer and cheese should align roughly in power.

ACIDITY: All cheeses have acidity—that's partly what preserves them—but some are tarter and tangier than others. Many goat-cheese recipes call for a long, slow fermentation that produces a lot of acidity. This tartness can make malty beers seem sweet and out of balance. Better to pair these tangy chèvres with highly hopped brews, such as IPAs; the hops bitterness can handle that tang. As for the increasingly popular sour ales, such as gueuze and Flanders red, try balancing their bold acidity with the sweetness of an aged Comté or Gouda.

SWEETNESS: Most cheeses that are more than a few days old have no measurable sugar because bacteria have converted all the lactose (milk sugar) to lactic acid. Nevertheless, many cheeses, especially aged cheeses, can leave a sweet impression. Think of the caramel and butterscotch notes in an aged Gouda or Coolea or the subtle *dulce de leche* sweetness of Garrotxa or Lamb Chopper. Many beers, in contrast, do have some residual sugar, while others merely seem sweet because of caramel notes from kilned (roasted) malt. Even if the sweetness is just a perception and not traceable to actual sugar, "sweet" beers and cheeses go well together. Malty brews such as porters and Maibocks, even when perfectly dry, pair seamlessly with cheeses that exhibit that hint of sweetness.

BITTERNESS: In cheese, bitterness is usually considered a flaw. In beer, it's part of the balance. Bitterness imparted by hops offsets the sweet, toasty nature of malt and keeps beer from being cloying. Some styles, like Belgian dubbels, have barely discernible bitterness. Others, like Imperial IPAs, grip your tongue. These bruisingly bitter beers can overwhelm many cheeses. High-acid Cheddars and sharp pecorinos—even peppercorn-laced pecorino—can put them in their place. Bitter beers are also your best bet with young, tangy goat cheeses, which rarely work with malty beers.

ALCOHOL: Pay attention to the alcoholic strength of a beer when you choose cheeses for it. Alcohol gives a beer body and staying power, that lingering sensation of flavor long after you swallow. The stronger the beer, the more likely it can manage concentrated, complex, or strong-flavored cheese. Cheeses aged for many months or even years—such as two- and three-year-old Goudas and Cheddars—appreciate beers of strength, and for all but the most mellow blue cheeses, high-alcohol beers should get the nod. Beers on the low end of the alcohol spectrum— quaffable brews like kölsch, British-style bitter, and many wheat beers—get along better with fresh cheeses and simple snacking cheeses that don't threaten them.

AROMA: Tantalizing aromas are among the most alluring features of both beer and cheese. Scents draw us in—or possibly repel us—and hint at the flavors to come. In beer, malts of many types produce aromas that range from bread dough to toasted grain, coffee, molasses, and chocolate. Hops, depending on the variety and when they're added to the beer, contribute many floral, piney, fruity, grassy, and spicy scents. Yeast can also leave signature aromas, such as banana and orange peel.

Cheeses, of course, have their own vast and complex aroma wheel, with scents attributable to pasture, molds, culture, and the enzymatic breakdown of fats and proteins. Young cheeses may smell of sour cream or fresh butter, while more mature cheeses develop aromas of toasted nuts, grass, caramel, mushrooms, or leaf litter. Aromatic harmonies between beer and cheese can deliver a lot of pleasure, as when a chocolate stout meets butterscotchy aged Gouda. What's not to like about *that* duo?

The following four guidelines distill the possibilities enough to get you started. Think of them as suggestions, not rules. Venture beyond them and, just as in real life, you'll find happy marriages that defy expectations.

Pair delicate beers with young, fresh cheeses.
    Example: Wheat beers or pilsners with young goat cheese, feta, burrata, or mozzarella.

Pair malty beers with nutty or "sweet" cheeses.
    Example: Bocks, Märzens, brown ales, stouts, porters, and holiday ales with aged alpine cheeses, Goudas, and other aged cheeses with nutty, buttery, or caramel aromas and a sweet finish.

Pair hoppy beers with tangy cheeses.
    Example: Pale ales and IPAs with goat cheeses and Cheddars.

Pair strong beers with blue cheeses and hard aged cheeses.
    Example: Imperial stouts, barley wines, and quadrupels with blue cheeses and aged sheep's milk cheeses.

BUYING, STORING, AND SERVING CHEESE

BUYING CHEESE

In more and more communities across the United States, consumers have access to knowledgeable cheese merchants. Some of these passionate cheesemongers operate tiny neighborhood shops and stock only a small, curated collection. Others oversee a broad inventory in a supermarket setting, where shoppers expect to find both an inexpensive Cheddar for macaroni and cheese and a pricey raw-milk farmstead Cheddar for a dinner party.

You will learn more about cheese, find a better selection, and take home better quality if you shop at a specialty-cheese store or a market with a staffed cheese counter. Supermarkets that sell only precut cheese for the grab-and-go shopper serve a purpose, of course, but they rarely stock the kind of variety and quality that make specialty cheese an adventure. If possible, identify a merchant in your community who cuts cheese to order, or who will at least offer a taste of a precut piece, so you can sample before you buy.

Ask questions at the cheese counter. How does this Wisconsin sheep's milk cheese compare to the Manchego you usually buy? Which of these blues is the boldest? Ask the merchant what cheeses he or she is excited about that day. A good cheese counter has a lot of turnover, with new cheeses coming in all the time, and the staff knows which wheels are tasting great and in peak condition.

Try to patronize a store that hires people with genuine enthusiasm for cheese and then trains them well. These savvy retailers offer you samples before you ask. They can tell you something about how the cheese was made or about the people who made it. And they can recommend other cheeses that will complement your selection on a cheese board. Make it a habit to buy at least one unfamiliar cheese each time you shop so your frame of reference continues to grow.

STORING CHEESE

Cheese will survive longer in your refrigerator if properly stored. When you return from the market, take a few moments to create a good home for your cheeses with the conditions they prefer. For most cheeses, that means changing the wrap. Cheeses hate plastic wrap because they can't breathe. Most cheeses are still releasing moisture, and if you trap that moisture with plastic, the cheese surface degrades. What's worse, many plastic films impart an unpleasant taste to the cheese's cut surface.

Some stores now use a breathable coated "cheese paper" to wrap cut pieces. If your purchases are so wrapped, leave them that way, but put them inside a lidded food-storage container. The container allows the cheeses to breathe while protecting them from the drying environment of the refrigerator.

If you purchase cheese wrapped in plastic film, remove the wrap when you get the cheese home. Rewrap in cheese paper (some cheese stores sell it), coated butcher paper, or wax paper, then place the cheese in a lidded food-storage container. You can put multiple cheeses in a single container, but store blue cheeses and stinky washed-rind cheeses separately. The blue mold and the washed-rind aromas can quickly infect other cheeses.

Hard cheeses such as Parmigiano Reggiano and aged Goudas have little moisture left to lose. They can be wrapped loosely in wax paper, then overwrapped tightly with aluminum foil. For these cheeses, you can dispense with the lidded container.

Change the wrap each time you take cheese out of the refrigerator. If mold tries to gain a foothold, simply cut or scrape it away. You don't need to discard the cheese.

No cut cheese improves in your refrigerator; it only declines. Try to buy only as much as you expect to use in the next few days. (Hard grating cheeses are an exception. They can survive unscathed in the refrigerator for weeks.) Cheeses also suffer from changes in temperature, so try to minimize the number of trips in and out of the refrigerator. If you expect to eat only part of a wedge, cut off that part and bring it to room temperature, but put the rest back in the fridge.

SERVING CHEESE

Cheese tastes best at room temperature and, with few exceptions, should be served that way. As the chill departs, the aroma blooms and the texture softens. Firm bloomy-rind and washed-rind wheels become supple inside, and their flavors emerge. Even hard cheeses become less waxy and brittle when allowed to warm slightly.

For a 1-pound piece, an hour at room temperature suffices. Bigger wedges may need a little longer. Take cold cheeses out of their wrap, put them on a tray or serving plate, and cover with a cake dome or inverted bowl so they don't dry out.

For safety, be cautious with super-moist products like cottage cheese, ricotta, and mozzarella. You can remove them from refrigeration for a half-hour or so before serving to take the chill off, but they should not remain at room temperature for long.

When assembling a selection of cheeses for guests, aim for diversity: a variety of milk types, shapes, rinds, textures, ages, and tastes. Juxtapose young, semisoft cheeses with hard, mature ones; delicate wheels with pungent ones; bloomy-rind disks with washed-rind types. Think about color and shape, too. An ash-coated goat log, a blue-veined wedge, and a washed-rind disk look more inviting together than three wedges with similar butter-colored interiors.

On the other hand, don't feel that you need a half-dozen selections to make an appetizing cheese course. A single cheese in perfect condition can make an impression, especially when paired with just the right beer.

When guests are serving themselves from a buffet or a passed tray, it's nice to provide a separate knife for each cheese. Observant guests will take the hint that the same knife shouldn't travel from the blue cheese to the goat cheese to the Brie. Leave rinds in place, when possible, as they are part of each cheese's beauty. At a stand-up gathering, where guests don't have implements, consider displaying a small piece with rind intact but cubing or slicing the rest into portions suitable as finger food.

STORING AND SERVING BEER

. . . .

STORING BEER

With most beers, fresh is best. Light, heat, and changes in temperature quickly extract a toll, staling or oxidizing bottled beers within weeks. As a rule, the lighter the beer (in both color and alcohol), the faster its decline. Highly hopped beers such as IPAs also lose vivacity quickly, as their hops aroma plummets with time. Drink 'em up! Dark beers and high-alcohol brews tend to have a little more stamina.

The death march accelerates in retail shops that display bottles near windows or under lights. Pay attention to the conditions in the stores where you shop. Think twice before buying a bottled beer that feels warm to the touch because of exposure to store lights or warm air. Despite the association of cans with low-end beer, several craft brewers have switched from bottles to cans to minimize the impact of light and extend their products' shelf life. At home, store beer in the refrigerator—preferably with the bottles standing up, to allow any yeast to settle to the bottom.

A few beer styles do reward extended storage if you can provide appropriate conditions: a dark, wine-cellar-like environment with steady temperatures near 55°F and humidity in the 50 to 70 percent range. High-alcohol brews such as strong ales, Imperial stouts, quadrupels, and barley wines are the best candidates for cellaring and may improve with a year's aging or even more. Some aficionados cellar them for a decade. The changes are hardly predictable, but many beers become more mellow and wine-like, with nutty or sherry-like aromas. Some people also enjoy putting away sour ales and bières de Champagne to experience the mellowing effects of time.

SERVING BEER

You're thirsty. The beer's in the fridge. You don't need a manual to tell you how to enjoy it. But if you're opening beer for aficionados, you'll probably want to observe a few of the niceties. Serving the beer at the appropriate temperature and pouring it properly into a suitable glass will not go unnoticed. And you'll probably soon become more finicky, too—and cranky when a craft beer isn't served with respect. These rituals aren't about one-upmanship, after all. They're about enhancing the drinking experience: how the beer looks, smells, and tastes.

The serving temperature: For most craft beers, the ideal serving temperature falls somewhere between "refrigerator cold" (38° to 40°F) and "cellar cool" (about 55°F). That's a sizable spectrum, almost 20 degrees, reflecting the diversity of beer styles and the differing needs of each. A pilsner served too warm or a porter served too cold loses a lot of charm.

So how do you determine where a particular style belongs on that serving-temperature spectrum? It isn't difficult, and you can put the thermometer away.

Bear in mind that chilling a beer makes it more refreshing but also mutes its fragrance. Thus, the lighter, more delicate beers that we appreciate as thirst quenchers—pilsner and kölsch, wheat beer, and some pale ales, for example—should be served at the cold end of the spectrum. Strong, dark beers such as Belgian-style dubbels, Imperial stouts, and barley wines belong at the other end, around 55°F. At that temperature, these aromatic brews flaunt their beguiling scents, heady concoctions of spice, dried fruit, and coffee. Most other beer types—from IPAs to sour ales—are content somewhere in the middle.

Here is a more detailed guide for the styles featured in this book, based on the recommended serving temperatures in *The Oxford Companion to Beer* (Garrett Oliver, editor).

38° TO 45°F
(refrigerator temperature)
American Pale Ale
Belgian-Style Pale Ale
Bière de Champagne
India Pale Ale (IPA) and Imperial/Double IPA
Kölsch and Blonde Ale
Pilsner
Wheat Beer

45° TO 48°F
(remove from the refrigerator about 15 minutes before serving)
Amber and Red Ales
Amber Lager and California Common
Bock and Doppelbock
Brown Ale
Maibock
Märzen and Oktoberfest
Saison and Bière de Garde
Sour Ale

48° TO 52°F
(remove from the refrigerator about 30 minutes before serving)
Belgian-Style Strong Golden Ale
Dubbel
Holiday Ales
Stouts and Porters
Tripel

52° TO 55°F
(remove from the refrigerator about 45 minutes before serving)
Barley Wine
Bitter and Extra Special Bitter (ESB)
Imperial Stout
Quadrupel

The glassware. Always use scrupulously clean glasses for beer. Even a smidgen of soap or fat residue can compromise head formation, the foamy cap that makes many beers so eye appealing. Sniff glasses to make sure they don't smell of detergent or stale cabinet. Glasses should be at room temperature—neither warm from the dishwasher, nor chilled. A frosty mug may be appropriate for a bland mass-market lager, but don't even consider it for a craft beer.

Just as wine connoisseurs might raise their eyebrows at being served Bordeaux in a Burgundy glass (but wouldn't refuse it), craft-beer fans associate certain beer styles with particular glass shapes. Most of these long-standing pairings have aesthetic or practical justifications. Pilsners, for example, look most beguiling in tall, flared flutes that show off their clarity and make room for the head. Fragrant Belgian-style ales call for stemmed goblets that taper inward to concentrate the aroma, allow for swirling, and contain the billowing foam.

You can invest in a variety of beer glasses if you want to be perfectly correct at all times. The pictures in this book will point you to the traditional glassware for each beer style. Alternatively, you can purchase a multipurpose glass like a stemmed tulip, which suits every type.

In any case, never allow the gaps in your glassware inventory to stop you from serving the beer you want. There's a strong argument to be made for the notion that the right glasses for any beer are the glasses you have.

The pour: Beer enthusiasts take a lot of pleasure in a well-poured beer, one with enough foam creation but not too much. Foam drives aromas up to your nose and releases some carbon dioxide, so the beer is less gassy and more creamy—a good thing, up to a point. Too much foam can rob the beer of carbonation and annoy a thirsty imbiber who has to wait for the head to subside.

Beers vary in their head-forming and head-retaining capability. High-protein beers such as wheat beers and highly carbonated brews like Belgian-style strong golden ale produce a lot of foam. (The Belgian ale Duvel is notorious for its frothy head.) Barley wines and bitters don't. But pouring technique also affects the volume of foam produced. Pour slowly onto the side of a tilted glass, and you will produce little or no foam. Pour steadily down the center of an upright glass, and admire the thick head you produce.

The most traditional pouring method calls for tilting the glass at a 45-degree angle. Pour slowly down the side of the glass until it is about three-quarters full. Then turn the glass upright and pour straight down the center to develop a head, taking care to leave any yeasty sediment in the bottle. For drinkers who like the sediment—some do—swirl the last remaining bit of beer in the bottle and pour it straight down the middle of the glass.

Despite major stylistic differences, many of the world's craft beers have at least one thing in common: They are ales. In contrast to lagers (page 72), ales are fermented with yeasts that prefer warm temperatures and that remain on top of the vat during fermentation. These yeasts work quickly, yielding beers that often have fruity or spicy aromas, brews that are ready to drink almost immediately.

America's craft brewers produce far more ales than lagers, in part because lagers require more time—they have to age—and more expensive equipment. The vast family of ales encompasses such diverse members as delicate kölsch, hoppy IPA, and malty, massive barley wine.

Top to bottom: Flagship Reserve, Cave-Aged Marisa

AMBER AND RED ALES

STYLE NOTES: A uniquely American category associated largely with West Coast breweries, amber ale makes the case for balance. Its malty sweetness, hops bitterness, and alcohol warmth blend seamlessly, with no single element clamoring for attention. Compared to the popular West Coast pale ales, ambers tend to be darker, richer, and maltier, with a more muted hops aroma and bite. These quaffable brews hover around 5 to 6 percent alcohol, in the midrange of the alcohol spectrum. Unlike many of the heavily hopped and high-proof ales from America's small-production breweries, amber ales shy away from extremes.

Oregon's Full Sail Brewing Company launched the amber ale phenomenon in 1989, but New Belgium Brewing's Fat Tire took the concept to the masses. Its success encouraged other brewers to try their hand at the style, making amber ales a lively American category. *Red ale,* a term popularized in the Pacific Northwest, is a variation on the amber-ale theme, with similar amber to copper color but often more ample hops and alcohol.

American hop varieties put their citrus, pineapple, and floral signature on amber ales alongside malty notes of biscuit and caramel. Expect moderate carbonation and a crisp, refreshing finish. Bitterness ranges from subtle to pronounced, with brews like Grand Teton's Pursuit of Hoppiness venturing into the hop-centric realm of an IPA. But with the exception of such outliers, amber and red ales are friendly beers, appreciated equally by the novice and the connoisseur. When you are unsure of your guests' beer preferences, amber ale is one choice that is likely to bridge a wide range of tastes.

BEERS TO TRY: Alaskan Amber; Anderson Valley Boont Amber; Bear Republic Red Rocket Ale; Bell's Amber Ale; Breckenridge Avalanche Ale; Eel River Organic Amber Ale; Full Sail Amber Ale; Grand Teton Pursuit of Hoppiness; Mendocino Brewing Red Tail Ale; New Belgium Fat Tire; North Coast Brewing Red Seal Ale.

CHEESE AFFINITIES: Cheeses with a hint of sweetness connect with the malty heart of an amber ale. For that experience, look to alpine and alpine-style cheeses like Beaufort, Gruyère, or Pleasant Ridge Reserve; to young cow's milk or goat's milk Gouda; or to France's sweet and nutty aged sheep's milk cheeses like Abbaye de Belloc. Mellow Cheddars have a nutty, well-integrated flavor that complements these balanced beers, although full-on tangy Cheddars will make amber ale seem sweeter. Even washed-rind cheeses can work if they aren't too pungent.

Point Reyes Farmstead Cheese **Toma,** a semifirm cow's milk wheel aged for about three months, has a warm-butter scent, a smooth and creamy mouthfeel, and the sweet finish of young Gouda. It isn't classic Gouda by any means—it more closely resembles young Asiago—but the cheesemaker borrows some Gouda techniques to produce a wheel with rich sour-cream flavor and muted acidity. It's hard to find a beer that doesn't go with this irresistible snacking cheese, but amber ale particularly responds to its sweet, buttery notes.

Inspired by the classic bandage-wrapped English Cheddars, Beecher's **Flagship Reserve** has a character all its own. The cheesemaker uses a nontraditional mix of cultures to give the cheese a creamier texture, nuttier aromas, and a gentler flavor than many Cheddars, without the typical tang. An aggressively hoppy IPA can handle Cheddar with more bite; but the brown-butter aromas and rounded flavors of Flagship Reserve appreciate a beer with a softer side.

Using milk from a Wisconsin cooperative, Carr Valley produces one of America's finest sheep's milk cheeses, **Cave-Aged Marisa**. Cheesemaker Sid Cook releases the 10-pound wheels after at least twelve months of aging, when they have a semifirm, golden interior and appetizing aromas of brown butter, mushrooms, wet stone, and hazelnuts. This mellow cheese is creamier than many aged sheep's milk wheels from Europe, with none of the lanolin scent that drives some people away from sheep cheese. Sweet, tart, and salty flavors merge seamlessly, leaving a balanced impression. A malty amber or red ale would complement Cave-Aged Marisa's buttery and nutty notes.

MORE CHEESES TO TRY: Abondance; Ardrahan; Arina Goat Gouda; Beemster XO; Cheshire; Comté; Lamb Chopper; Meadow Creek Grayson; MouCo ColoRouge; Parmigiano Reggiano; Petit Agour; Pilota; Pleasant Ridge Reserve; Roth Käse Gruyère Surchoix; Tumalo Farms Fenacho or Rimrocker; Wisconsin Sheep Dairy Cooperative Dante.

Left to right: Keen's Cheddar,
Mezzo Secco, Pondhopper

AMERICAN PALE ALE

STYLE NOTES: For many craft-beer enthusiasts, American pale ales offer the most appealing integration of hops, malt, and alcohol. Typically, these brews exhibit plenty of up-front hops aroma without being aggressively floral or piney. They finish with brisk bitterness, but never enough to curl your tongue. Malt shores up the middle, yet they don't smell sugary or finish sweet. They have enough alcohol to give them body—typically, 4.5 to 6 percent alcohol—but not enough to make them unwise at lunch. Carbonation is usually moderate, on the cusp of crisp and creamy.

Pale ales have proven so popular with consumers that most American craft breweries have released one at some point. Although patterned after English pale ales, the American efforts tend to be bigger and brassier, often with the citrusy scent of American hops, some grassy notes from dry hopping (steeping hops in the beer after fermentation to extract aromatics), and higher alcohol.

These well-balanced ales are "pale" only in relation to the dark ales that prevailed in the days when malt roasting was more primitive and less controllable. Pale ales range in color from deep gold to pale amber to burnished copper. Many if not most are filtered and clear, but some are unfiltered and consequently hazy.

BEERS TO TRY: Bell's Pale Ale; Boulevard Pale Ale; Deschutes Mirror Pond Pale Ale; Firestone Walker DBA (Double Barrel Ale); Grand Teton Sweetgrass APA; Great Divide DPA (Denver Pale Ale); Moylan's Tipperary Pale Ale; North Coast Brewing Acme Pale Ale; Oskar Blues Dale's Pale Ale; Sierra Nevada Pale Ale; Stone Brewing Pale Ale.

CHEESE AFFINITIES: Although pale ales are impressively versatile and don't clash with many cheeses, they shine with cheeses that are as full flavored and balanced as they are. Turn to firm cheeses with the savoriness and concentration that emerge with age, such as Cheddar and Manchego. Pale ales stand up to cheeses with herbs and spices, especially peppercorns, but many blue cheeses seem to rob these ales of some sparkle. And young, soft, buttery cheeses like triple-creams and robiolas tend to be overshadowed by pale ale's robust hoppiness.

Mezzo Secco, from California's Vella Cheese Company, resembles a young Dry Jack, this creamery's better-known hard cheese. Produced from raw cow's milk and matured for three to four months, a wheel of Mezzo Secco has a thin rind rubbed with oil and black pepper. The interior is pale gold, semifirm, and smooth, with aromas that hint of nuts and hay, and mild, milky flavors. Neither pungent nor particularly rich, Mezzo Secco doesn't tire the palate, so you can happily keep snacking until the beer is gone.

Produced on a family farm in Somerset now in its fourth generation, **Keen's Cheddar** is as traditional as English Cheddar gets. The Keens insist on using raw cow's milk from their own herd, a culture derived from local microflora, and animal rennet for the coagulant. When the wheels are only a few days old, they are wrapped in muslin and coated with lard—another practice that defines traditional Cheddar—to protect them until a rind forms. For top quality, look for wheels selected by Neal's Yard Dairy, the London exporter. A fine wheel of Keen's has a handsome natural rind; a golden, slightly waxy interior that smells of nuts, grass, and earth; and a tangy acidity that synchs with pale ale's hoppy bite.

From Oregon's Tumalo Farms, a specialist in Gouda-style goat cheese, the goat's milk **Pondhopper** loves a pale ale. No surprise there, as the fresh curds are actually steeped in a hoppy Oregon pale ale before being drained, molded, and pressed. After a three-month maturation, the 9-pound wheels have a smooth, semifirm, supple interior and inviting aromas of yeast, caramel, and cooked milk. (Alas, the cheese does not smell of hops.) Pondhopper's creamy texture and pleasing balance of sweetness and salt make it easy to like and a good companion for many beer styles, but pale ale may head the list. The ale's malty center responds to the cheese's mellow nature, while the beer's bitterness keeps the match from being cloying.

MORE CHEESES TO TRY: Bellwether Farms Pepato; Chimay; Grafton Village Four-Year Cheddar; Leiden; Montgomery's Cheddar; Manchego; Point Reyes Toma; Tumalo Farms Capricorns; Twig Farm Goat Tomme.

BARLEY WINE

STYLE NOTES: In barley wine, ale reaches its apex of richness, complexity, and strength. Don't be misled by the name: Barley wine is beer by any measure. But at 8 to 12 percent alcohol, it approaches wine in power. Some call it the brewer's answer to port, a beverage for sipping contemplatively at the end of a winter meal, preferably fireside. Like port, it benefits from aging. Even a few months in a bottle will soften it and bring its components into better balance. With longer aging, barley wines can develop some of the nutty aromas of sherry.

Barley wine's birthplace is England, but production is dwindling there. In contrast, American craft brewers have embraced the style and several festivals are devoted to it, a sign of barley wine's popularity among brewers and consumers.

Barley wines range considerably in color, from deep gold, to amber or copper with a ruby glint, to dark brown. They tend to be clear and viscous, leaving "legs," or a drippy film, on the glass, and they rarely produce much of a head because of this syrupy texture. What they do offer is full-on toffee, toast, and roasted-grain aromas from the lavish use of malt, and sometimes dried-fruit aromas like dried cherries and plums. American versions are reliably more hoppy than their English equivalents, but all classic barley wines emphasize bitterness over malt. They tend to finish dry, with brandy-like warmth.

Brewery names for barley wine (sometimes spelled "barleywine") often include the word *old,* possibly a reference to the cellaring that many undergo. With its pioneering Old Foghorn, introduced in 1975, San Francisco's Anchor Brewing Company is widely credited with popularizing barley wine in the United States.

BEERS TO TRY: AleSmith Old Numbskull; Anchor Brewing Old Foghorn; Avery Brewing Old Jubilation Ale; Burton Bridge Thomas Sykes Old Ale; Deschutes Mirror Mirror; Dogfish Head Olde School; Fuller's Golden Pride; Great Divide Old Ruffian; Green Flash Barleywine; Moylan's Old Blarney Barleywine Style Ale; Sierra Nevada Brewing Bigfoot.

CHEESE AFFINITIES: You can bring out the big guns with barley wine, such as smoked or washed-rind cheeses with room-filling aromas. But you don't have to match the beer's power with pungency. Voluptuous triple-cream cheeses provide a pleasing textural echo, and buttery blue cheeses love barley wine's silkiness. Or pay homage to the style's roots in Britain and pair with a classic farmhouse Cheddar. Aged cheeses with pronounced roasted-nut or caramel aromas, such as aged Goudas, also shine with barley wine.

Simon Jones, the English creator of **Lincolnshire Poacher,** was inspired by his country's great Cheddars when he developed his own cheese in the early 1990s. Produced with raw milk from his own cows, Jones follows the traditional Cheddar procedures to yield a 45-pound wheel with obvious similarities to the classic Somerset Cheddars—but differences, too. Lincolnshire Poacher has the firm, dense, creamy-yet-crumbly texture of great Cheddar, with a brown-butter aroma and caramel-like sweetness. Pair it with barley wine for a completely satisfying dessert.

The California triple-cream, washed-rind **Red Hawk** has that niche almost to itself. Most triple-cream cheeses have bloomy rinds, and few washed-rind cheeses are made with cream-enriched milk. So Cowgirl Creamery's Red Hawk deserves praise for originality but even more acclaim for its ultra-creamy texture and seductive mushroom fragrance. Unwrap a whole Red Hawk and leave it at room temperature for a day, covered with an inverted bowl, to allow the flavor to blossom. Barley wine complements the cheese's luscious texture and matches it in strength.

Made in Vermont from raw cow's milk, Jasper Hill Farm's **Bayley Hazen Blue** is among America's most celebrated blue cheeses. A farmstead cheese—meaning it is produced on the farm exclusively with milk from that farm—Bayley Hazen Blue has a natural rind and the cylindrical shape of a French Fourme d'Ambert. But seventy-five days of aging in the farm's underground cellar give this cheese its distinctive texture and flavor: creamy yet a little crumbly, straddling the line between moist and dry; with nutty and meaty aromas and a smoky, bacon-like finish. The creamery says some wheels develop a licorice character. More mellow than piquant, Bayley Hazen Blue still wants a strong partner. A powerful barley wine meets it head on, and the beer's toastiness and dried-fruit aromas envelope this buttery blue.

MORE CHEESES TO TRY: L'Amuse Gouda; Boerenkaas; Cabot Clothbound Cheddar; Roelli Dunbarton Blue; Isle of Mull; Keen's Cheddar; La Peral; Old Amsterdam; Rogue River Blue; Rogue Smokey Blue; Stichelton; Stilton.

Top to bottom: Bayley Hazen Blue, Lincolnshire Poacher, Red Hawk

CHEESE FOR DESSERT

OMMEGANG
THREE PHILOSOPHERS

Conclude a winter evening with a trio of rich and concentrated cheeses and accompany them with Three Philosophers. This unusual blend of malty ale and Belgian kriek is the beer equivalent of a chocolate-covered cherry. Hinting of praline, dark chocolate, and dried fruit, this potent brew may keep the conversation going into the wee hours. Serve with butterscotch-scented aged Gouda; the luscious French triple-cream Délice de Bourgogne; and the silky Swiss mountain cheese Challerhocker, and no one will miss the pastry.

Top to bottom: Délice de Bourgogne, L'Amuse Gouda, Challerhocker

Left to right: Widmer's Brick, Camembert

BELGIAN-STYLE PALE ALE

STYLE NOTES: Despite the similarity of the names, Belgian-style pale ales and American pale ales are distant kin at best. Think of the two styles as cousins rather than siblings. Unlike American pale ales with their full-blown hoppy scent, Belgian-style pale ales owe most of their fragrance to Belgian yeast strains. The fruity aromas typically produced by these yeasts include orange peel, banana, and pear, with sometimes a hint of sour cherry. Some, like the famous Orval, rely on *Brettanomyces* yeast to add a subtle sourness and complexing aromas of earth and barnyard.

Amber to copper in hue, Belgian-style pale ales have a more malty personality than their American counterparts. Even so, the malt aspect is delicate, closer to toasted grain or baking-powder biscuits than to caramel. European hop varieties contribute a restrained malt-balancing bitterness, a component heightened dramatically in Belgian IPAs like De Ranke XX Bitter.

Most Belgian-style pale ales finish dry, although the brewer may have used sugar to elevate the alcohol without enriching the body. At 5 to 7 percent alcohol, these brews have more power than their easy drinkability suggests. They are a little too potent to think of as session beers, yet one refreshing glass invites another. Moderate in every respect, they don't wear out their welcome.

BEERS TO TRY: De Koninck; De Ranke XX Bitter (Belgian IPA); Green Flash Rayon Vert; Ommegang BPA; Ommegang Rare Vos; Orval Trappist Ale; Saranac Belgian Style Ale; Palm Spéciale; Svea (Belgian IPA).

CHEESE AFFINITIES: With their fruity aromas, brisk carbonation, spicy flavors, and dry finish, Belgian-style pale ales share some attributes with hard cider. So it's no stretch to pair these brews with the cheeses that cider complements, such as aged British farmhouse cheeses like Cheddar, Cheshire, and Caerphilly; or with Camembert, a cheese made in cider country. These well-balanced beers can also handle washed-rind cheeses that aren't too feisty.

Created by a Swiss immigrant in the 1870s, Brick cheese has a distinguished history in Wisconsin. Sadly, modern plants have largely abandoned the old recipe in favor of a bland cheese that hardly resembles the pungent original. Only Widmer's Cheese Cellars continues to produce a Wisconsin Brick of distinction. Overseen by third-generation cheesemaker Joe Widmer, **Widmer's Brick** has the signature sandwich-loaf shape, the sticky bacteria-washed rind, and the fruity, beefy, yeasty fragrance that old-timers expect. The name comes not from the cheese's shape but from the bricks used to press the fresh curds—the same bricks Joe Widmer's grandfather used. Widmer's Brick is relatively tame for a washed-rind cheese, and an ale like Orval, with its high alcohol and its own touch of funk, can stand ground against it.

Using cow's milk from their own small herd, the Kirkham family makes Great Britain's most esteemed and traditional Lancashire. Ruth Kirkham and her son, Graham, perpetuate the recipe Ruth learned from her mother, making **Mrs. Kirkham's Lancashire** the only one still produced with raw milk and animal rennet. Instead of waxing the wheels, as other Lancashire producers do to prevent moisture loss, the Kirkhams wrap their wheels in muslin and coat them with butter. This practice protects the rind while allowing the wheel to breathe and develop flavor. The unusual procedure also calls for combining curd from several days, a step that heightens the crème fraîche aroma and lemony tang. But the most distinctive feature of Kirkham's Lancashire is its tender texture, as buttery and crumbly as shortbread. That lemon-butter quality creates a bridge to Belgian-style pale ale with its own fruity bakeshop scent.

The French **Camembert** sold in America often disappoints, lacking the big, mushroomy fragrance and buttery texture of the finest raw-milk Camembert in France. Food and Drug Administration regulations prohibit the sale of raw-milk Camembert because it hasn't aged long enough, a minimum of sixty days. But celebrated French *affineur* (cheese ager) Hervé Mons, working with a Normandy cheesemaker, has managed to produce what long seemed impossible: an aromatic and supple Camembert from pasteurized milk. Packaged under his name or the brand name Le Pommier, this Camembert develops a room-filling scent of mushrooms, garlic, and barnyard. Its aromas mesh with the fruity, spicy fragrance of Belgian-style pale ale, and the Camembert's silky texture loves the beer's vigorous effervescence.

MORE CHEESES TO TRY: Appleby's Cheshire; Ardrahan; Brie de Nangis; Caerphilly; Chaource; Coulommiers; Cowgirl Creamery Red Hawk; Crave Brothers Les Frères; Scharffe Max; Sweet Grass Dairy Green Hill; Tomme de Savoie.

BELGIAN-STYLE STRONG

Left to right: Mt. Tam, Chimay, Beaufort

GOLDEN ALE

STYLE NOTES: Pale yet potent, with alcohol levels that often top 10 percent, Belgian-style strong golden ales can ambush the unsuspecting. Because these brews can resemble delicate pilsners visually, with flavors to match, many drinkers don't see the punch coming. No wonder so many strong golden ales sport names that suggest the underworld, as if to signal the danger therein. Savor them slowly.

Duvel (Flemish for "devil") is the undisputed pack leader and one of the most admired brews in Belgium. Whether from that country or the United States, most other strong golden ales emulate Duvel to some degree. The style relies on pale, lightly kilned malts, yielding a beer of pilsner-like color, rarely darker than pale gold. Fruity aromas dominate, with any malty character in the background. Instead, look for the banana, citrus, and pear notes typically produced by Belgian yeast strains, perhaps with hints of ginger, clove, and spice cake.

Most brewers add candi sugar to augment the alcohol without adding body, so these strong ales sit surprisingly lightly on the tongue. They typically open sweet but finish dry, with Champagne-like carbonation. Hops contribute some balancing bitterness but little or no aroma. Strong golden ales resemble Belgian-style tripels but tend to be crisper and dryer.

Properly poured, strong golden ale generates a thick, frothy head. Custom calls for serving the beer in a thick-stemmed goblet to accommodate that generous foam.

BEERS TO TRY: Avery Brewing Salvation; Bière de Belœil; Brooklyn Local 1; Duvel; Lucifer; Jolly Pumpkin Oro de Calabaza; North Coast PranQster; Russian River Damnation; SAXO; Unibroue Don de Dieu; Victory Brewing V-12.

CHEESE AFFINITIES: The alcoholic strength of these ales makes them good partners for aged cheeses with concentrated flavors. Consider alpine cheeses similar to Comté or Cheddars that are more mellow than tangy. Many of these beers make a sweet impression that links them to cheeses with caramel notes, such as Goudas. Strong golden ales have enough vigor for milder washed-rind cheeses, and their palate-scrubbing effervescence appreciates the soothing contrast of a silky triple-cream cheese.

France's **Beaufort,** a hefty alpine wheel resembling Swiss Gruyère, amply rewards the cheesemaker's patience. The finest wheels receive at least twelve months of aging, and eighteen months is not too long. Over that time, the massive rounds are washed repeatedly with brine to nurture the hard rind and encourage flavor-enhancing bacteria. Gradually, the internal paste becomes firmer; its color deepens from ivory to gold; and the flavor and aroma intensify. Made in the Savoie region from raw cow's milk, a well-aged Beaufort matches strong golden ale in power and offers similar fruity and spicy notes. It melts on the tongue, leaving behind a nutty sweetness and an intoxicating scent of toasted hazelnuts, brown butter, buttered toast, and dry-aged beef.

Not a country renowned for its cheeses, Belgium nonetheless produces at least one wheel that perfectly complements its strong golden ales: the famous **Chimay**. Created by Trappist monks from raw cow's milk, Chimay Grand Cru weighs about 4½ pounds and receives about two months of aging, with repeated brine washings, before release. Under its thin orange rind is a semisoft, springy, butter-colored interior with mild eggy and earthy aromas. On the spectrum of stinky washed-rind cheeses, Chimay occupies the mellow end. It doesn't need an alcoholic monster to tame it, but it does want a muscular beer with enough effervescence to counteract its dense creaminess.

Cowgirl Creamery's **Mt. Tam,** a plush cow's milk triple-cream, cushions the tongue-tingling carbonation of strong golden ale. Many triple-cream cheeses have a lactic, sour-cream tang that clashes with strong ale's gentle sweetness, but not Mt. Tam. Its unusual recipe calls for washing the curd, a procedure that yields a sweeter, less acidic cheese. A fully ripe Mt. Tam has an interior as spreadable as buttercream frosting, with a mild and buttery taste. A younger Mt. Tam may retain a firm core, but the cheese will still welcome the ale's palate-refreshing bubbles.

MORE CHEESES TO TRY: Abondance; Appenzeller; Beehive Cheese Promontory; Bleu des Basques; Bleu Mont Cheddar; Le Maréchal; Raclette; Tumalo Farms Capricorns; Montagne du Jura; Pilota.

BIÈRE DE CHAMPAGNE

STYLE NOTES: Somewhere on the spectrum between beer and Champagne, between the working stiff's draught and the beverage of swells, lies bière de Champagne. A new style that originated in Belgium and has made a splash in the United States, bière de Champagne offers beer lovers an ale worthy of life's big moments.

Every beer has bubbles, but bière de Champagne has more. This hybrid beverage marries conventional beer ingredients—malted grain, water, hops, and yeast—with the *méthode champenoise,* the time-consuming and laborious process behind every fine sparkling wine. So after its initial fermentation, and possibly a second fermentation in tank, the beer undergoes yet another fermentation with more yeast in a thick-walled Champagne bottle. After months of aging, the bottles are riddled, or slowly upended over several weeks to force the yeast into the neck. Finally, the bottles are disgorged to remove the spent yeast, just as for fine sparkling wine; topped up with additional beer; and resealed with a Champagne-style cork and wire hood.

Poured into a flute—the ideal way to serve it—a pale golden bière de Champagne foams luxuriously and unleashes a vigorous mousse. At 10 to 12 percent alcohol, these costly brews have a rich, full body and a racy scent that leaps from the glass. Thanks to the Belgian yeast, their aromas lean heavily to fruit and spice, with hints of orange blossom, apricot, apple, ginger, lemongrass, and mulled wine. They don't show much malt character or hops bitterness, seducing instead with lively effervescence, heady fragrance, and an off-dry finish.

Currently, the limited offerings in this category come from two Belgian breweries and one pioneering American producer, the Boston Beer Company. But the level of consumer interest in bière de Champagne suggests that this tiny niche will surely grow.

BEERS TO TRY: Boston Beer Company (Samuel Adams) Infinium; DeuS Brut des Flandres; Malheur Brut Réserve.

CHEESE AFFINITIES: A luxurious triple-cream cheese is a slam-dunk match for fizzy bière de Champagne. The beer's mighty carbonation helps scrub the palate clean between tastes of velvety cheese. Mellow, creamy blue cheeses also appreciate bière de Champagne's bubbles and hint of sweetness, and hard aged cheeses with caramel or butterscotch notes jibe with the beer's fruit and spice.

From New York State, Nettle Meadow Farm's **Kunik** unites goat's milk with Jersey cow cream to yield an original and luscious triple-cream cheese. Weighing about 12 ounces, Kunik offers a plush and spreadable off-white interior underneath its bloomy rind. The delicate aroma hints at clotted cream and cultured butter; the flavor is similarly subdued, with a muted nuttiness and no goaty tang. This cheese seduces with its richness and voluptuous texture, the ideal foil to a brisk and bubbly bière de Champagne.

L'Amuse Gouda, a 30-pound wheel matured by Dutch cheese merchant Betty Koster, demonstrates the impact of *affinage* (expert aging). Koster hand-selects young wheels from Beemster, a Dutch producer, and then nurtures them at her aging facility near Amsterdam for two years. On release, they are sublime, with a gem-like amber color; a firm, waxy paste dotted with protein crystals; and an aroma that marries butterscotch with whiskey. A nugget melts on the tongue, leaving the impression of a salted caramel. Bière de Champagne matches this fine Gouda in complexity and special-occasion stature, and the beer's cider-like fruitiness rounds out the cheese's burnt-sugar notes.

A cow's milk wheel from northern Italy, **Piave** attains its peak of flavor when matured for six to twelve months. These older wheels, known as Piave Vecchio (aged Piave), develop a dense, firm texture similar to a young Parmigiano Reggiano. With aromas of toasted walnuts and butterscotch, Piave has a concentrated, caramel-like sweetness. It stops short of the candy-sweet intensity of L'Amuse, yet it shares the Gouda's synergy with sassy, spicy bière de Champagne.

MORE CHEESES TO TRY: Bleu des Basques; Bleu du Bocage; Cashel Blue; Chaource; Jasper Hill Bayley Hazen Blue; Jasper Hill Constant Bliss; La Peral; Rouge et Noir Triple Crème Brie; Nancy's Hudson Valley Camembert; Parmigiano Reggiano; Roaring Forties Blue; Seal Bay Triple Cream Brie.

Left to right: Piave, Kunik

PACIFIC NORTHWEST FEST

DESCHUTES BREWERY
MIRROR POND PALE ALE

America's premier hops-growing region is also a hotbed for handcrafted cheese. This matchup celebrates both. Savor the fragrance of the local Cascade hops in Mirror Pond Pale Ale and the talent of Oregon and Washington cheesemakers in this foursome: a creamy bloomy-rind chèvre (Dutchman's Flat); a Gouda-style goat cheese (Pondhopper); an aged cow's milk wheel (Brindisi); and a mellow cow's milk Cheddar (Flagship Reserve).

Left to right: Pondhopper (2 pieces); Brindisi (2 pieces); Flagship Reserve; Dutchman's Flat

BITTER AND

Top to bottom: Landaff,
Hook's Cheddar, Wagon Wheel

EXTRA SPECIAL BITTER

STYLE NOTES: For many British people and for Anglophiles everywhere, the "pint of bitter" defines the pub experience. Modest in alcohol, the beer won't derail your afternoon if you have one for lunch, and countless hardworking blokes have a couple of pints at the end of the day with no harm done. That explains their reputation as session beers, a sensible choice for a long evening with friends.

An English or English-style bitter is fundamentally a pale ale with the volume turned down: less alcohol, less malt character, lower IBUs (a measure of bitterness). Despite the name, these brews aren't particularly hoppy or bitter (although American versions can be more hop forward). The "bitter" moniker arose as a way for customers and publicans to distinguish these draught brews from sweeter, less-hopped mild ales.

The style parameters are broad in this category, but a classic bitter showcases British hop varieties. Less blatantly aromatic than most American types, British hops contribute more subdued aromatics, often described as fruity, earthy, or resiny. Some American craft brewers use English hops in their bitters and ESBs in a nod to the style's origins, but they may incorporate the more citrusy American hops, too.

Bitters are easy-drinking beers, with low carbonation and only about 3.5 percent alcohol. They are more common on draught than in bottle, and it is standard practice in pubs to serve them at cellar temperature, not chilled. From a Best Bitter, Special Bitter, or Extra Special Bitter (ESB), expect more alcoholic strength, malty aroma, and bitterness, but even these brews rarely surpass 6 percent alcohol or approach the tongue-gripping bitterness of an IPA.

In the glass, bitters and ESBs tend to have an amber or copper hue with sparkling clarity. Malt makes the first aromatic impression, often with notes of toffee, light caramel, toast, cereal, or crackers and sometimes a bitter-orange or woodsy scent. Malty sweetness gives way to a dry and moderately bitter finish, with the piney, fruity signature of English hops.

BEERS TO TRY: AleSmith Anvil Ale ESB; Coniston Brewing Bluebird Bitter; Fuller's ESB; Fuller's London Pride; Great Lakes Brewing Moondog ESB; Morland Old Speckled Hen; Pretty Things Hedgerow Bitter; Samuel Smith's Old Brewery Pale Ale; Yards Brewing Extra Special Ale; Young's Bitter.

CHEESE AFFINITIES: Bitters and ESBs are beers of relatively low strength and complexity and fare best with cheeses that are similarly easygoing. Cheeses with bold, pungent, or sharp flavors can dominate these beers, making them taste thin and watery. Instead, look to mild, approachable cheeses made for everyday consumption, cheeses with sweet, buttery, or nutty flavors that are easy to like.

The 25-pound **Wagon Wheel** is the largest cheese produced by Cowgirl Creamery, a California dairy that made its name with the petite cow's-milk Red Hawk and Mt. Tam. Modeled loosely on Asiago, Wagon Wheel is a pressed-curd, natural-rind cheese from organic cow's milk, matured for two to three months. The butter-colored, semifirm interior has a buttery aroma with a hint of the barnyard fragrance of Italian Fontina. The flavors are well balanced and mellow, and the cheese melts well. A grilled-cheese sandwich made with Wagon Wheel would be a feast with an ESB.

New Hampshire's Landaff Creamery produces its Old World–style cheese from the raw milk of its own Holstein cows. Modeled after Caerphilly, a cheese of Welsh origin that is mostly made in England today, the 9- to 10-pound wheels of **Landaff** spend three to four months in the aging cellars at Jasper Hill Farm in Vermont. This carefully monitored maturation, or *affinage,* produces a handsome mold-cloaked natural rind over a pale gold, semifirm interior. The texture is open and crumbly; the aroma redolent of butter, cave, and earth. Like Caerphilly, Landaff offers a bright lemony tang that harmonizes with the piney aromatics of English hops.

Hook's Cheddars are among Wisconsin's finest cheeses, especially the batches that receive extra aging. These 40-pound block Cheddars mature slowly in vacuum-sealed bags so they never develop a rind, but they do gain complexity over time. A five-year-old Hook's Cheddar will be creamy and utterly smooth, with just a hint of a bite. After seven to ten years, the cheese will deepen in flavor, diminish in tang, and develop some of the crunchy protein crystals typical of Parmigiano Reggiano; at that mellow stage, it pairs beautifully with a lightly malty ESB. The fifteen-year-old Cheddar, sometimes for sale at the creamery's booth at the Dane County (Madison) Farmers' Market, is a flavor sensation.

MORE CHEESES TO TRY: Beehive Promontory; Caerphilly; Capriole Julianna; Cougar Gold; Garrotxa; Hook's Seven-Year Sharp Cheddar; Juniper Grove Farm Tumalo Tomme; Keen's Cheddar; Matos St. George; Midnight Moon; Montgomery's Cheddar; Point Reyes Toma.

BROWN ALE

STYLE NOTES: Easy-drinking and mellow, with malty flavors foremost, brown ale has deep roots in England. Over time, distinctive regional styles have emerged there. Southern English brown ales are sweeter and milder than their northern counterparts but have a dwindling share of the market. The northern English style—paler, stronger, and dryer—has more fans in England today and is also the approach that most American craft brewers emulate, albeit in their own freewheeling way. Some craft-beer enthusiasts consider brown ale to be relatively insipid, but at a few small enterprises like Tampa's Cigar City—home of the Oatmeal Raisin Cookie Brown Ale—the style is inspiring brews that are a long way from bland.

Interpretations vary widely, but brown ale is always malt focused. Based on pale malts, many formulas also incorporate darker malts to deepen the beverage's color and complexity. Most brown ales are clear, with a dark amber, copper, or light brown hue. Toasted grain, caramel, nut, and toffee aromas are common; some brown ales smell like warm baked bread. Chocolate malt, a heavily roasted malt with the color of dark chocolate, gives some of these beers a scent suggesting cocoa or cold coffee. Classic brown ales have little to no hops aroma and low hops bitterness, but American versions tend to be hoppier. A few American brewers even dry-hop brown ale—steeping additional hops in the beer after fermentation—to boost hops aroma and bitterness.

Brown ales typically range between 5 and 6 percent alcohol. They don't have a long shelf life and are meant to be consumed fresh. These are beers for quaffing, not for pondering, to enjoy, perhaps, when you're in the mood for a malty brew but for a beverage less heavy than a porter.

BEERS TO TRY: Anchor Brewing Brekle's Brown; Avery Brewing Ellie's Brown Ale; Brooklyn Brewery Brooklyn Brown Ale; Cigar City Maduro Brown Ale; Grand Teton Bitch Creek ESB (Extra Special Brown); Lost Coast Downtown Brown; Midnight Sun Brewing Kodiak Brown Ale; Rogue Ales Hazelnut Brown Nectar; Samuel Smith's Nut Brown Ale; Shipyard Brewing Brewer's Brown Ale; Sierra Nevada Tumbler; Tilburg's Dutch Brown Ale.

CHEESE AFFINITIES: Brown ale's nutty and toffee aromas and relative lack of bitterness make for harmony with cheeses that have similar toasty, brown-butter notes and mellow character. Alpine and alpine-style cheeses such as Comté, Beaufort, and Pleasant Ridge Reserve are good candidates. Also look to Goudas and aged sheep's milk cheeses that are more nutty than piquant. For example, the caramel-scented Abbaye de Belloc is likely to be more compatible than a peppery Fiore Sardo, although both are aged wheels made from sheep's milk.

Tête de Moine, a Swiss washed-rind cheese made from raw cow's milk, traces its origins back eight centuries to a monastery in the Jura Mountains. In the aftermath of the French Revolution, the monks abandoned the monastery, and local citizens took over the cheese making. Today, several Swiss dairies produce this silky, semifirm cheese. Produced in a cylindrical form, taller than it is wide, Tête de Moine is traditionally shaved, not sliced. A cheese plane will do the job, but purists use a *girolle,* a manual slicer that creates beautiful ruffled sheets as it scrapes the surface in circular fashion. Matured for about three months, Tête de Moine offers mingled aromas of fried shallots, roasted peanuts, and dry-aged beef and a sweetness that appreciates the malty flavors of brown ale.

Wisconsin cheesemaker Marieke Penterman, a Dutch immigrant, makes superb Dutch-style Goudas with the raw milk of her own herd of Holsteins. Following the Dutch practice of seasoning Gouda with spices, Penterman adds whole fenugreek to one of her cheeses to produce what she has christened—using the Dutch spelling—**Marieke Foenegreek Gouda.** A frequent prize winner, Penterman's Gouda has a creamy texture and a mellow, nutty, faintly mustardy taste that a toasty brown ale complements. Matured for two to six months, the cheese becomes firmer and fuller flavored as it ages.

Spain's most famous cheese, **Manchego,** derives its name and its mouth-filling flavor from the rich milk of Manchega sheep. Producers ship the cheese at a range of maturities, and its personality grows more complex with time. At three to six months, the aroma suggests sour cream, cultured butter, or cheesecake. Give it six more months and the wheel will have a nuttier aroma, like warm brown butter; a lingering sweetness; and a dryer, more granular texture. A Manchego of any age paired with brown ale hits some of the same sensory notes as buttered toast, but a mature cheese will deliver the most satisfaction.

MORE CHEESES TO TRY:
Abbaye de Belloc; Abondance; Beehive Cheese Promontory; Cantal; Central Coast Creamery Holey Cow; Coolea; Durrus; Everona Piedmont; Fontina Val d'Aosta; Gabiétou; Gruyère; Ombra; Ossau-Iraty; Pecorino Toscano (aged); Pleasant Ridge Reserve; Stilton; Winchester Gouda (medium aged); Zamorano.

**Top to bottom: Tête de Moine,
Marieke Foenegreek Gouda,
Manchego**

Top to bottom: Mimolette, Morbier

DUBBEL (DOUBLE)

STYLE NOTES: Belgium's Trappist monks devised the recipe for dubbel, a strong version of brown ale, with 6 to 8 percent alcohol. Dubbels typically have a rich, complex, malt-centered personality and a copper or caramel color. Most are bottle conditioned—refermented in the bottle—so they may not be crystal clear. Hops remain in the background, contributing little to the aroma and only a barely perceptible bitterness in the finish. Instead, dubbels seduce with bakeshop aromas such as raisin, clove, molasses, brown sugar, dried fig, toffee, and toast.

These seductive scents result largely from caramelized liquid sugar added to the wort, a common practice for Belgian brews. The sugar deepens the beer's color, contributes toffee-like aromas, and helps boost alcohol without adding heaviness.

Expect creamy, medium carbonation from a dubbel and a medium-full, almost viscous body from the elevated alcohol. The first impression on the palate is typically malty sweetness, but most dubbels finish crisp and dry. Some, like Ommegang Abbey Ale, have a lingering sweetness, with a bitter edge for balance.

BEERS TO TRY: Achel 8°; Allagash Dubbel; Anderson Valley Brother David's Double; Captain Lawrence St. Vincent's Dubbel; Chimay Red Cap (Chimay Première); Maredsous Brune; New Belgium Abbey Ale; Ommegang Abbey Ale; St. Bernardus Prior 8; Westmalle Dubbel.

CHEESE AFFINITIES: With their malty richness and lush texture, dubbels can accompany cheeses with robust flavor. Consider washed-rind cheeses of moderate pungency; truly smelly cheeses may prove too much. Alpine cheeses with their nutty scent and silky textures and aged Goudas with their caramel notes can be especially pleasing partners for dubbels.

Made in Holland for Cypress Grove Chevre, a California creamery, **Midnight Moon** may surprise tasters who think they don't like goat cheese. Wheels weigh about 10 pounds and are aged for six months or more, yielding a firm, rinded cheese with a dense, shaveable interior—not the spreadable texture associated with younger goat cheese. Midnight Moon blends the sweetness of aged goat Gouda with the brown-butter, toasted-nut, and caramel aromas reminiscent of aged Gruyère—flavors that align nicely with a malty dubbel.

Mimolette's vivid pumpkin-orange color draws attention at the cheese counter, where it stands out among the paler selections. Even Wisconsin Cheddars, tinted with the same plant-based dye, do not have quite so strident a hue. Modeled after Dutch Edam, this French cow's milk cheese looks like a flattened bowling ball and only develops an interesting character with considerable age. At eighteen to twenty-four months, Mimolette becomes brittle and waxy, with a butterscotch aroma and a piquant, sweet-salty taste that welcomes a strong, spicy dubbel in response.

The ribbon of ash in the middle of a **Morbier** is largely decorative now, but in times past, it served a purpose. French farmers made curds with the evening milk and sprinkled them with ash to protect them and prevent a rind from forming. The following day, they would top the ash with curd from the morning milk to complete the wheel. Today, this practice probably persists only on a handful of small farms. Most Morbier, a cow's milk cheese, is made on a large scale and is not particularly compelling. But when hand-selected and matured in the cellars of one of France's esteemed *affineurs* (cheese agers), such as Jean d'Alos or Pascal Beillevaire, Morbier becomes a cheese to relish. A semisoft, washed-rind cheese weighing 11 to 18 pounds, a good Morbier has a supple ivory interior with many small openings and aromas of mushroom, earth, and damp cellar—plenty of character to merit a matchup with a powerful dubbel.

MORE CHEESES TO TRY: Appenzeller; Beemster XO; Chimay; Comté; Central Coast Creamery Holey Cow; Garrotxa; Hoch Ybrig; Leiden; L'Etivaz; Lincolnshire Poacher; Marieke Gouda; Meadow Creek Grayson; Munster; Murcia Curado (Naked Goat); Pleasant Ridge Reserve; Raclette; Spring Brook Farm Tarentaise; Vacherin Fribourgeois.

HOLIDAY ALES

STYLE NOTES: Many craft brewers around the world unleash their creative juices at holiday time, producing a flood of uniquely styled Christmas ales. Typically strong and richly malty, and often smelling of gingerbread spices and citrus peel, these heady brews seem intended to match the season's party spirit. They hark back to the Belgian tradition of thanking brewery patrons at year's end with an especially festive creation. Today, Christmas ales are often bottled in large format, an acknowledgment that many are destined for parties or gifts.

Some enthusiasts sock these brews away—if high in alcohol, they may improve with age—but producers intend them for winter enjoyment, preferably shared among friends around a blazing hearth.

Belgian breweries and the American craft brewers inspired by them typically rely on dark roasted malts and baking spices such as clove and coriander to give these beers color and personality. A few are moderate in strength, but most have some extra holiday spirit, and a tally of 9 to 12 percent alcohol is not uncommon. They range from dark amber to chocolate-brown and often have spice-cake, dried-fruit, caramel, licorice, or whiskey aromas and sometimes a touch of barnyard funk. Most are showcases for malt and offer little or no hop fragrance, but exceptions abound. Sierra Nevada Celebration Ale is a classic IPA, with a big hop aroma and no spicing whatsoever.

From the more traditional holiday ales, expect moderate to high effervescence, which helps those bakeshop aromas to bloom. High alcohol can give these beers a viscous mouthfeel, although bitterness should balance that sweet impression. Some finish dry, perhaps with cider-vinegar or sour-cherry tartness; others are noticeably sweet, even syrupy. In the United States, Anchor Brewing initiated the Christmas ale custom. Like many breweries, Anchor alters the recipe for its Christmas Ale every season, so each vintage is unique.

Some brewers use the term *winter warmer* for their high-proof year-end ale. That nomenclature nods to British brewing tradition and the notion of wassail, a spiced, sweetened, and warmed ale to chase away chills or at least help you forget them. Winter warmers tend to be dark, malty, strong, and spiced, but interpretations vary.

BEERS TO TRY: Anchor Brewing Christmas Ale; Delirium Noël; De Struise Tsjeeses; Fantôme de Noël; Gouden Carolus Noël; Grand Teton Brewing Coming Home Holiday Ale; Port Brewing Santa's Little Helper; Saison Dupont Avec Les Bons Vœux; Scaldis Noël; St. Bernardus Christmas Ale.

CHEESE AFFINITIES: Pair these strong, spicy ales with robust cheeses, especially aged wheels with toasted-nut or caramel flavors that harmonize with the spice. Aged Goudas, with their butterscotch and whiskey aromas, marry well with these beers; so do aged sheep's milk cheeses that have brown-butter scents. Buttery blue cheeses with nutty notes are a good choice for spiced holiday ales with a sweet edge. In the spirit of holiday indulgence, consider triple-cream cheeses. Their plush, buttery texture complements the viscosity of these high-alcohol beers.

More approachable than the peppery Cabrales, Spain's more famous blue cheese, **Valdeón** still makes a strong statement. At its best, this leaf-wrapped cow's milk blue from northern Spain has a creamy, melting texture and a bold, spicy, but not biting flavor. At the cheese counter, ask for a taste and leave the Valdeón behind if it is overly salty or sharp. Wait for a more buttery, nutty wheel that doesn't curl your toes. A strong holiday ale has enough intensity and power to handle this substantial, mouth-filling cheese.

Comparable to the popular P'tit Basque but tastier and made on a more artisanal scale, **Petit Agour** showcases the quality of sheep's milk from the French Pyrenees. At just under 2 pounds, it resembles a miniature Ossau-Iraty, the prized sheep's-milk cheese from France's Basque region. Its roasted-nut and caramel aromas and concentration bring Gruyère to mind, although the underlying flavor is indisputably sheep's milk. A handsome natural rind protects Petit Agour's smooth, semifirm, straw-colored interior. Shaving the paste with a cheese plane releases even more of its brown-butter fragrance, a scent that finds a complement in the toffee-like sweetness of many holiday ales.

Its gorgeous amber color and salted-caramel flavor make **Saenkanter** a near-universal favorite. Like other aged Dutch Goudas, this 28-pound cow's milk wheel darkens in color and develops a seductive butterscotch aroma with sufficient time in the aging cellar. Saenkanter spends three years in the care of a Dutch *affineur,* an expert in maturing cheeses. All that patience yields a wheel with a hard, crumbly interior studded with crunchy protein crystals; a caramel fragrance that may remind you of whiskey or oloroso sherry; and a long sweet-and-salty finish. It's a dessert cheese, certainly, and appealing with a complex, high-alcohol holiday ale that can match its prodigious flavor.

MORE CHEESES TO TRY: Abbaye de Belloc; Berkswell; Bleu d'Auvergne; Bleu des Basques; Blu del Monviso; Brillat-Savarin; Cowgirl Creamery Mt. Tam; Gouda (aged); Ombra; Parmigiano Reggiano; Roelli Dunbarton Blue; Roomano Pradera; Tomme Brûlée; Wilde Weide Gouda; Winchester Gouda.

Top to bottom: Petit Agour, Valdeón

INDIA PALE ALE

Top to bottom: Pepato, Humboldt Fog

AND IMPERIAL OR DOUBLE IPA

STYLE NOTES: British brewers get the credit for fashioning the first IPAs, now the most popular of craft-beer styles in America. During the height of the British Empire, brewers prepared their pale ales for the long sea journey to India by brewing them stronger and with extra hops. The elevated alcohol and hops gave these ales more longevity, so they were still refreshing when they arrived, months later, in steamy India.

Modern American craft brewers have embraced and adapted the style, using Pacific Northwest hops to create highly perfumed beers with forward floral, citrus, pineapple, and pine aromas and a palate-scrubbing bitterness. American hops tend to have more essential oils than European hop varieties, so the ales brewed with them are more blatantly aromatic. Dry hopping—steeping additional hops in the beer after fermentation—gives most IPAs an even more effusive aroma. Malt aroma and flavor remain low-level players in most IPAs, contributing just a suggestion of toasty sweetness.

Today, many American craft breweries produce an IPA because consumers can't get enough of this thirst-quenching style. West Coast brewers tend to make their IPAs more floral and hop forward than East Coast and Midwest brewers, who let the malt speak a little more.

Imperial IPA, often called Double IPA, raises the volume on the IPA style by employing even more hops to heighten the floral and grapefruit aromas and the bitterness. Imperial IPAs are often more alcoholic than a classic IPA, too, but it is the tongue-gripping bitterness that any drinker will notice first.

BEERS TO TRY: India Pale Ale (IPA): Anchor Brewing Liberty Ale; Ballast Point Big Eye IPA; Bear Republic Racer 5 IPA; Boulevard Brewing Single-Wide IPA; Dogfish Head 60 Minute IPA; Founders Brewing Centennial IPA; Great Divide Brewing Titan IPA; High Water Brewing Hop Riot; Lagunitas Brewing Lagunitas IPA; Rubicon Brewing India Pale Ale; Russian River Brewing Blind Pig IPA; Victory Brewing HopDevil. **Imperial (Double) IPA:** Brooklyn Blast!; Dogfish Head 90 Minute IPA; Firestone Walker Double Jack; Full Sail Brewing Elevation; Lagunitas Brewing Hop Stoopid; Oskar Blues G'night Imperial Red; Russian River Brewing Pliny the Elder; Stone Ruination; Victory Brewing Hop Wallop.

CHEESE AFFINITIES: The up-front bitterness of many IPAs and Imperial IPAs makes them particularly palate refreshing, a welcome "chaser" for creamy and high-fat cheeses, such as triple-creams. Their bold personality stands up to moderately strong cheeses, including spiced cheeses that might overwhelm lighter brews. Their bitterness can handle the tang of English-style Cheddars and the bright acidity of young goat cheese better than most beer styles.

The bloomy-rind **Humboldt Fog** from California's Cypress Grove Chevre is a style icon among American goat cheeses, its fine ripple of gray ash amid a chalk-white paste making it instantly recognizable. The goat cheese's dense, palate-coating texture and lively acidity challenge many beers, especially malty styles, but an IPA or Imperial IPA welcomes the task. The scrubbing quality of an IPA slices through the cheese's chalky firmness and balances its tangy acidity to perfection.

Fiscalini Bandage-Wrapped Cheddar, patterned after the finest British Cheddars, is matured in cheesecloth (the "bandage") instead of wax, so it breathes as it ages. Made with raw cow's milk from Fiscalini's own herd, this California farmstead cheese spends at least eighteen months in the creamery's aging room, developing the classic crumbly-waxy Cheddar texture and profound nutty and grassy aromas. The snappy bite of hops in an IPA or Imperial IPA counters the Cheddar's lingering tang.

Bellwether Farms Pepato was inspired by the black pepper–laced pecorinos of Tuscany, but this California version is intentionally moister, less salty, and more mellow. Made with raw sheep's milk, laced with whole peppercorns, and matured for about three months, wheels of Pepato exhibit a floral, peppery scent mingled with aromas of lamb chops and wet stone. The flavor is moderately piquant, the finish tart and tangy. The bitterness in IPA and Imperial IPA complements this cheese's spicy bite.

MORE CHEESES TO TRY: Appleby's Cheshire; Bleu Mont Bandaged Cheddar; Cabot Clothbound Cheddar; feta; Fontina Val d'Aosta; Garrotxa; Hook's 10-Year Cheddar; Juniper Grove Farms Dutchman's Flat; Keen's Cheddar; Kirkham's Lancashire; Leiden; Matos St. George; Montgomery's Cheddar; Mt. Townsend Trailhead; Tumalo Farms Capricorns; Vella Dry Monterey Jack; Wensleydale.

**Left to right: Picandou,
Fleur Verte**

KÖLSCH AND BLONDE ALE

STYLE NOTES: Crisp and zippy, with the refreshing prickle of high carbonation, kölsch finds its way into many hands on hot days. Resembling a pilsner in its easy drinkability, it shines in settings that call for a brew with a light touch: at brunch, at the beach, or with an *insalata caprese* at lunch.

An authentic kölsch comes only from Germany and specifically from the city of Cologne, where it originated as a competitor to Czech pilsner. Brewed anywhere else, it isn't true kölsch but a kölsch-style beer or blonde ale, the name many brewers use for beers of this style. To many tasters, the differences will be negligible, but a kölsch-style beer, by tradition, should incorporate at least some German hop varieties, while blonde ale is not so restricted.

Pale straw in color, with awesome clarity, kölsch and blonde ale deliver flavor without weight. Everything about them is delicate and dialed back: They have little or no hops aroma, a muted bitterness, and a soft base of sweet, biscuity malt. Some have faintly fruity aromas, like white wine. They are lean and gentle on the palate, and their finish is fresh and dry. Typically under 5 percent alcohol, kölsch and blonde ale make excellent session beers and a good starting point for newcomers to craft beer who aren't accustomed to the intense flavor of some other styles.

BEERS TO TRY: Alaskan Brewing Summer Ale; Deschutes Twilight Summer Ale; Mission Brewery Blonde Ale; New Belgium Brewing Somersault Ale; Reissdorf Kölsch; Rogue Ales Oregon Golden Ale; Russian River Brewing Aud Blonde; Saint Arnold Brewing Fancy Lawnmower; Samuel Adams East West Kölsch; Ska Brewing True Blonde Ale; Sünner Kölsch.

CHEESE AFFINITIES: Many American craft breweries release their kölsch-style and blonde ales in early summer, with references to warm-weather icons like sandy beaches, porches, and lawn mowers. Accordingly, pair them with the fresh, light cheeses that are so inviting in summer, like ricotta, farmer's cheese, cottage cheese, feta, fresh goat cheese, mozzarella, and burrata. Even a simple lunch of cottage cheese with tomatoes and cucumbers is an excuse to open a kölsch or blonde ale.

The diminutive **Picandou** looks like a chalk-white hockey puck and is just the right size for a single serving. A young, rindless goat cheese from France, it has a smooth, soft texture, like natural cream cheese, and a fresh, lemony flavor. Drizzle it with olive oil and bake it just until it quivers, then serve the cheese on a nest of baby greens. Its gentle tang elevates the malty sweetness of a kölsch or blonde ale, and the cheese's creaminess softens the beer's carbonation.

California's small Central Coast Creamery produces **Holey Cow,** a Baby Swiss with far more character than most cheeses in that uniquely American category. Matured for at least two months, the 10-pound cow's milk wheels develop dime-sized eyes and a big, buttery aroma with hints of sour cream, salted butter, and custard. Use a cheese plane to shave thin slices for a sandwich or a cheese plate. The flavor is concentrated and sweet, but simple and not too robust for a mild kölsch or blonde ale.

An herb-coated French goat cheese, **Fleur Verte** ("green flower") smells like a Provence hillside on a hot summer day. Dried thyme, tarragon, and crushed pink peppercorns coat the exterior, and the scalloped edges on this 5-pound wheel give it a whimsical daisy-like shape. It leaves the creamery when it is only four days old, so Fleur Verte is still moist and delicate when it arrives on American shores. Under its green cloak is a chalk-white interior with a vivid herbaceousness and a lemony finish. Accompany with a salad or grilled vegetables and a chilled kölsch or blonde ale for a perfect summer lunch.

MORE CHEESES TO TRY: Bellwether Farms Crescenza; Calabro Ricotta; Cowgirl Creamery Clabbered Cottage Cheese; Franklin's Teleme; Mt. Vikos Barrel-Aged Feta; mozzarella; Primo Sale; Redwood Hill Cameo; Vermont Butter & Cheese Fresh Crottin.

QUADRUPEL

STYLE NOTES: The potent beers that merit the quadrupel designation can rival wine in alcoholic strength, with some brews reaching 12 percent alcohol. No wonder people refer to quadrupels (quads, for short) as "sleeper" beers. They are surprisingly easy to drink for such massive beverages, and their inebriating effects can sneak up on you.

Like dubbels and tripels, quads derive from the brewing traditions of Belgium's Trappist monasteries. At the Belgian abbeys and breweries that produce quads—among them, Chimay and Rochefort—the beers are likely to be the strongest in the lineup. They tend to be dark hued, ranging from amber to the color of over-brewed tea, due in part to the addition of dark liquid sugar to the wort. This sugar adds alcohol potential without adding heaviness, and in some brews, it contributes a brown-sugar scent and some residual sweetness.

Brewers may use a complex blend of grains in quad formulas, perhaps incorporating wheat, oats, or rye in addition to a variety of barley malts. Quads are all about the malt; most offer little or no hops aroma and just a suspicion of bitterness. Even so, they are profoundly aromatic, mingling scents of dried cherry, plum, raisin, dried fig, fruitcake, gingerbread, and caramel. Highly carbonated but not biting, they produce a huge, creamy head in the glass. And while they may exhibit spicy aromas, actual spices are not part of the brew.

Some brewers don't use the term *quadrupel,* preferring instead a proprietary name, often including a number that hints at alcoholic strength. Belgium's Rochefort 10 and St. Bernardus Abt 12 are examples of this phenomenon, but don't assume that the number correlates precisely with alcohol content. Rochefort 10, for example, is even stronger than 10 percent alcohol. (The numbers are a holdover from an old system of measuring potential alcohol.) Chimay Grande Réserve has all the qualities of a quadrupel, but the abbey does not use the term. "Belgian dark strong ale" is another way of characterizing such beers.

Like barley wines, which have similar alcoholic strength, quadrupels can improve with bottle aging. Under the proper conditions, they can be cellared for several years, becoming less sweet, more complex, and even more wine-like in their aromas.

BEERS TO TRY: Avery Brewing The Reverend; Chimay Grande Réserve (Chimay Bleu); Deschutes Brewery The Stoic; Malheur 12; Ommegang Three Philosophers; Rochefort 10; St. Bernardus Abt 12; La Trappe Quadrupel.

CHEESE AFFINITIES: Beers of such large stature complement cheeses with bold personality, such as blue cheeses, washed-rind cheeses, and hard aged cheeses such as Cheddars and Goudas. Cheeses with nutty aromas or silky cooked-milk sweetness (common in alpine cheeses such as Comté, Beaufort, and Gruyère) are particularly compatible with these plummy and malt-forward beers.

Switzerland's **Gruyère** receives a minimum of five months' aging, but the best wheels are nurtured much longer. Made with raw cow's milk, these giant wheels—they can weigh 60 pounds or more—become nuttier and more intensely savory with time. A twelve- to eighteen-month-old cave-aged Gruyère can be a spectacular taste experience, far more compelling than the supermarket Gruyère many consumers purchase for cooking. With a scent of hazelnuts and brown butter, a silky texture, and a sweet finish, aged Gruyère needs a malt-focused beer and has enough concentration to face a quadrupel.

Wheels of Dutch Gouda can be bland and uninspiring when young, but two to three years of cellar aging transforms them. They develop irresistible aromas of butterscotch, toffee, and whiskey; a creamy, almost fudgy interior dotted with crunchy protein crystals; and a mellow, candy-like sweetness. **Beemster XO,** an extra-aged Gouda from a century-old Dutch cooperative, fits that description and finds an echo in a malty, plummy quadrupel.

Invented in the 1970s, England's **Shropshire Blue** has an obvious kinship with the much older and better-known Stilton. Made in the same forms as Stilton, and at some of the same creameries, Shropshire Blue resembles England's most famous blue cheese in every way but color. The pumpkin color of the paste, or interior, of Shropshire Blue comes from the addition of annatto, the harmless and relatively tasteless plant-based dye that also tints some Cheddars and Goudas. Like Stilton, Shropshire Blue has nutty aromas, a mellow flavor, and a creamy, buttery texture, all qualities complemented by a heady, spice cake–scented quadrupel.

MORE CHEESES TO TRY: Bayley Hazen Blue; Chimay; Fourme d'Ambert; Grafton Village Red Vask; Marieke Gouda; Roth Käse Grand Cru Gruyère Surchoix; Pleasant Ridge Reserve; Roelli Dunbarton Blue; Saenkanter; Stichelton; Stilton; Valdeón; Wilde Weide Gouda.

Shropshire Blue

SOME LIKE IT STRONG

NAPA SMITH
BONFIRE IMPERIAL PORTER

With an aroma like Turkish coffee and plenty of alcoholic warmth and spice, Napa Smith Bonfire Imperial Porter is a brew for thrill seekers. Gather a few friends who like extreme sports and sample this potent beverage with cheeses that won't shrink before it: the bold and buttery Caveman Blue; the coffee-rubbed Barely Buzzed; and the lush, cream-enriched Kunik.

Top to bottom: Kunik, Caveman
Blue, Barely Buzzed

Left to right: St. George, Fromage de Meaux, Fontina Val d'Aosta

SAISON AND BIÈRE DE GARDE

STYLE NOTES: In the days before refrigeration, Belgian farmers in the country's French-speaking southern region would brew *saison* ("season") ales in the spring for consumption through the summer, or until cold weather made it possible to brew again. Today, brewers make saisons year-round, but the image persists of these beers as so-called "farmhouse ales," everyday nourishment for Belgian farm families and their crews, a welcome part of the daily provisions, probably savored with sturdy bread and strong cheese.

Saison brewing almost died out in Belgium, but the style is resurgent, with the esteemed Brasserie Dupont leading the way. American craft brewers are fleshing out the category with their own interpretations, which tend to be more highly hopped than their Belgian counterparts.

In keeping with their origins as summer beers, saisons promise refreshment. They are typically moderate in alcohol (although American renditions often top 8 percent), with fine and vigorous effervescence; a thick, fluffy head; a mid-range level of bitterness; and a dry, snappy finish. They range from pale gold to amber, and many are cloudy from bottle conditioning, the practice of naturally carbonating beer by adding a little fresh yeast and sugar to each bottle.

Belgian saisons are brewed largely with pilsner malts and rarely have more than a light malt aroma. American brewers sometimes include darker malts and other grains such as rye or oats. You can expect some hops aroma, but it won't be aggressive; more common are fruity scents such as green apple, pear cider, banana, and orange peel. American brewers sometimes add seasonings such as coriander, dried orange peel, or black pepper to the brew, but any spicy notes in the beer should be subtle. Saisons tend to start sweet on the palate and finish dry, although a few have an intentionally sour finish. Overall, saisons are balanced, lightly spicy, easy-drinking beers that can handle a wide range of cheeses.

The French counterpart to Belgian saison is *bière de garde* ("beer for keeping"), a style that originated from the same need: to produce a beer in late spring capable of lasting through the summer, when hot weather made brewing a challenge. Alcohol and hops both act as preservatives, so bières de garde were typically stronger and hoppier than the usual brew.

Although more alike than different, these two styles diverge in a few ways worth noting. Saison recipes typically call for saison strains of yeast, responsible for the spicy and fruity scents. Bières de garde, in contrast, often rely on wild yeasts and may show more earthy, funky, wooden-barn smells. Saisons tend to be dryer, while bières de garde are typically maltier and sweeter. Both encompass a wide style spectrum, ranging in color from blonde to amber to brown. Expect the darker saisons and bières de garde to be maltier and higher in alcohol than brews identified as *blonde*.

BEERS TO TRY: The Bruery Saison Rue; Castelain Blond Bière de Garde; De Glazen Toren Saison D'Erpe-Mere; Gavroche French Red Ale; Jolly Pumpkin Bam Bière; Lost Abbey Red Barn Ale; North Coast Brewing Le Merle; Ommegang Hennepin; Pretty Things Brewery Jack D'Or; Saison Dupont Vieille Provision; Stillwater Stateside Saison; Upright Brewing Seven.

CHEESE AFFINITIES: In many respects, saisons and bières de garde are medium-intensity beers, with aromatic complexity and moderate alcoholic strength, but without high-volume bitterness, malty sweetness, or heat. These beers pair best with cheeses that have similar intensity—neither too little, nor too much. Saisons and bières de garde are a little too big and spicy for delicate, fresh cheeses like Crescenza or young chèvres. And the two beer styles lack the malty richness that complements highly concentrated cheeses like aged Comté and Gouda. But almost any cheese in that vast middle ground will be happy with saison or bière de garde. Silky soft-ripened wheels with mushroom aromas—cheeses in the Brie and Camembert family—are particularly well suited to these brews.

St. George from California's Matos Cheese Factory is a three-month-old cow's milk wheel with a natural rind; a sturdy, waxy, golden interior; and many tiny eyes. Created by Portuguese immigrants in imitation of a cheese from their homeland, the Azores, St. George has an aroma that mingles warm butter and grass and a pleasing acidity that stops short of Cheddar-like tang. Its flavor is mouth-filling and well developed, but not huge, comparable in palate impact to a saison or bière de garde.

Northern Italy's **Fontina Val d'Aosta** is not only a treasured cooking cheese—stirred into risotto, sliced on top of polenta, or melted for *fonduta,* the region's fondue—but a delightful table cheese that pairs perfectly with saison or bière de garde. Made from raw cow's milk and matured for three to four months, wheels of Fontina Val d'Aosta are repeatedly turned and washed with brine during their aging. This step discourages some exterior molds and encourages the formation of a thin crust. Underneath the crust is a semifirm, supple, butter-colored interior with a few small eyes and the aroma of roasted peanuts and herbs. The flavor is nutty and mellow, becoming stronger with age.

France's beloved Brie de Meaux can't enter the United States because it doesn't meet the FDA's aging requirements for raw-milk cheese. To replace it, French creameries have devised **Fromage de Meaux,** similar but for the use of pasteurized milk. When ripe—tan striations on the rind and a slight give to gentle pressure are two clues—this thin bloomy-rind wheel will have a supple, spreadable texture and aromas of black truffle and butter. A blonde saison or bière de garde will match the cheese's moderate intensity, and the beer's high carbonation will cut through the buttery richness. Both a spicy saison and a more earthy bière de garde will find a complement in this mild, mushroomy cheese.

MORE CHEESES TO TRY: Abbaye de Belloc; Capriole Sofia; Castelbelbo; Jasper Hill Harbison; Nancy's Hudson Valley Camembert; Parmigiano Reggiano; Pierre Robert; Point Reyes Toma; Rogue Creamery TouVelle; Seal Bay Triple Cream Brie; Sweet Grass Dairy Green Hill; Tomme de Savoie; Vermont Butter & Cheese Cremont.

Top to bottom: Nancy's Hudson Valley Camembert, Wensleydale, Crescenza

SOUR ALES:
WILD ALE, LAMBIC, GUEUZE, FLANDERS RED ALE, AND FLANDERS BROWN ALE

STYLE NOTES: What's so appealing about sour beer? The very idea makes some drinkers recoil, but tart, even vinegary ales have a long history and many fans. These controversial brews can skirt the edge of respectability, with aromas so funky that no cheese can tame them, or with gripping acidity that stops just shy of vinegar.

Modern Belgian brewers have refined the production of sour ales, but the style has ancient roots. Before commercial yeast strains made fermentations predictable, brewers were at the mercy of wild microflora. Yeasts and bacteria naturally proliferating in the air, on brewery walls, or in wooden casks would ferment the wort's sugars, with often unpredictable results. These so-called **"wild ales"** might have earthy, horsey, or leathery aromas if *Brettanomyces* yeast played a role; or a rhubarb-like tartness if ambient bacteria converted the wort's malt sugar to acid.

Over centuries, brewers devised techniques to make these ales more palatable—by blending casks, or softening the sourness with fruit, or mellowing the character by aging. Today, Belgian brewers and the American brewers inspired by them produce sour ales in a variety of traditional styles, including lambic, gueuze, and Flanders red and brown ales. These beverages are among the most complex, peculiar, and oddly compelling examples of the brewer's craft.

True Belgian **lambic,** a dry, unblended beer made by spontaneous fermentation, is rare in the United States. Far more common is **gueuze** (pronounced, roughly, GER-zuh), a blend of young and old lambics. These beers range from golden to amber to peach-skin red, and they may be cloudy from bottle conditioning (intentional refermenting in the bottle) or clear. Don't look for hop aromas or bitterness. The lambic procedure relies on aged hops, which no longer have much aromatic or bittering potential but do help preserve the beer. Lambics and gueuzes can age in barrel or bottle for years.

Gueuzes are moderate in alcohol but highly effervescent, with aromas that may startle the unprepared. Swirl a glass and expect to release scents of earth, barnyard, lemonade, green apple, cider vinegar, or even decaying apples. The flavor is likely to be brisk, bone dry, and mouth-puckering.

Adding fruit to a lambic gives this style another dimension. To make **kriek** (cherry lambic) or **framboise** (raspberry lambic), fresh fruit is added while the lambic is still in barrel, prompting a new fermentation. When fully dry, the ale is drained off the fruit pulp and may or may not be sweetened before bottling. Traditional Belgian kriek has a rosy hue; fruity aromas mingled with the typical lambic funk; teeth-rattling acidity; and a lively, Champagne-like mousse. Sweetened kriek can taste like cherry soda. If it's the dry style you're after, look for the word *oude* (old) or *tradition* on the label.

Flanders red ale and Flanders brown ale resemble lambics in their bone-jarring tartness, but don't rely on spontaneous fermentation. Instead, brewers inoculate the wort with yeasts and bacteria selected to produce the desired acidity and wine-like notes. Sometimes called "the Burgundy of Belgium," Flanders red ale typically has a dark copper or deep amber color, with aromas of plum, peach, dried cherry, raspberry, citrus, sherry vinegar, and caramel. These ales persist on the palate with a sour grip.

From Flanders brown ale expect a darker, reddish-brown hue and more malty toffee notes mingled with the scent of sour cherry, raisin, and balsamic vinegar.

Neither of these Flanders styles is heavy or high in alcohol, but they happily bring up the rear in a meal. More Madeira-like than Burgundian, they excel as an end-of-meal digestif.

BEERS TO TRY: Bacchus; Cantillon Lambic; Cuvée des Jacobins Rouge; Deschutes Brewing The Dissident; Duchesse de Bourgogne; Goose Island Lolita; Hanssen's Artisanaal Oude Kriek; Jolly Pumpkin La Roja; Lindemans Gueuze Cuvée René; Monk's Café Flemish Sour Ale; New Belgium Brewing La Folie; Rodenbach Grand Cru; Russian River Brewing Consecration; Russian River Brewing Sanctification; Russian River Brewing Supplication; St. Louis Gueuze Fond Tradition.

CHEESE AFFINITIES: Their vigorous carbonation and palate-scrubbing acidity make sour ales like gueuze an appealing contrast with triple-cream cheeses. These beers can also balance the sweetness of cheeses with caramel notes, such as aged Gouda. Or pair them with young, rindless fresh chèvre to echo the beer's acidity, or with moist, fresh cow's milk cheeses, like Teleme, that have a sour-cream tang. Some tasters find harmony between the funky barnyard aromas in some wild ales and similar aromas in washed-rind cheeses, such as Epoisses, but that's a risky pairing. The human nose is easily overwhelmed. As for fizzy, highly sweetened fruit lambics, think of them as refreshment, perhaps, but not as good partners for cheese.

Nancy's Hudson Valley Camembert marries cow's milk with sheep's milk in a luscious cheese that can take the place of dessert. From New York's Old Chatham Sheepherding Company, this bloomy-rind, double-cream disk may resemble a French Camembert on the outside, but the interior is far more plush and velvety. The cheese's palate-coating richness appreciates the vigorous carbonation of sour ale, and its mild, salted-butter flavor lets the sour ale lead the dance.

From California's Bellwether Farms, the cow's-milk Crescenza looks like a soft, floppy disk of pizza dough. Like Italian Stracchino, its inspiration, Crescenza tastes best soon after it is made. The creamery releases this 2- to 3-pound square at less than a week old, when it smells like crème fraîche and has a soft, spreadable, yielding texture. An assertively malty or hoppy beer would overwhelm Crescenza's fresh tartness and delicate, buttery flavor, but gueuze matches its lively acidity.

Traditional Wensleydale is a sophisticated and respectable British cheese made by a centuries-old Yorkshire creamery. Ignore the tricked-out variations laced with cranberries and pineapple—they are made by the same creamery but for a less discriminating audience—and look for Wensleydale with a natural rind, exported by the esteemed Neal's Yard Dairy. These handsome 8- to 10-pound wheels, produced from pasteurized cow's milk, spend three to four months in an aging cellar, developing aromas of cheesecake and caramel. The moist, semifirm interior has a smooth, creamy texture and a tart, cultured-milk tang that marries well with sour ale's sprightly tartness.

MORE CHEESES TO TRY: Brillat-Savarin; Franklin's Teleme; Jasper Hill Farm Constant Bliss; Epoisses; Leiden; Marieke Cumin Gouda; Mimolette; Nicasio Valley Foggy Morning; Murcia Curado (Naked Goat); Pierre Robert; Point Reyes Toma; Tumalo Farms Pondhopper; Tumalo Farms Rimrocker.

STOUT, PORTER, AND IMPERIAL STOUT

STYLE NOTES: Stouts and porters owe their dark color and layered aromas to deeply roasted barley malt. The hues on these brews range from over-steeped tea to inky espresso, and their alluring scents elicit descriptors like toast, toffee, raisins, molasses, coffee, Kahlúa, and chocolate. Despite these dessert-like aromas, porters and stouts often (but not always) finish dry.

Many of these beers exhibit little or no hops aroma, although American stouts and Imperial stouts may show some. Moderate hops bitterness helps balance the mouth-filling malt, and a little bitterness may also come from the heavy roasting. Some recipes even incorporate roasted coffee beans or brewed coffee. For oatmeal stout, the brewer adds a small portion of oats to the grist, the ground grains that supply the sugar for fermentation. Oats contribute a particularly creamy texture to the finished brew and help generate a fluffy, voluptuous head the color of café au lait.

The term *stout* derives from stout porter, historically a stronger, more alcoholic rendition of traditional English porter. The typical English or American porter is moderate in alcohol, in the 4 to 5 percent range, and modern stout is often not much stronger. But Imperial stout, sometimes called Russian Imperial stout, is another matter. These massive brews are often quite potent, from 8 to 12 percent alcohol, and everything else about them verges on extreme, too. They can look almost like chocolate syrup, opaque and mysterious, with a thick foam the color of an espresso's *crema*. Expect heady, spirituous aromas, perhaps mingling dried fruit, coffee liqueur, vanilla, and bittersweet chocolate—a panoply of scents as sensuous as a chocolate-covered raspberry. An Imperial stout is a fireside beer for a cold winter's night and an ideal companion for robust cheeses.

BEERS TO TRY: Stout and Porter: AleSmith Speedway Stout; Bear Republic Big Bear Black; Boulevard Brewing Bully! Porter; Carnegie Porter; Deschutes Brewery Black Butte Porter; Dogfish Head World Wide Stout; Eel River Brewing Organic Porter; Firestone Velvet Merlin Oatmeal Stout; Founders Brewing KBS (Kentucky Breakfast Stout); Fuller's London Porter; Marin Brewing Point Reyes Porter; Meantime Brewing Coffee Porter; Moylan's Dragoons Dry Irish Stout; Samuel Smith's Oatmeal Stout; Samuel Smith's Taddy Porter; Sierra Nevada Porter.

Imperial Stout and Imperial Porter: Brooklyn Brewery Black Chocolate Stout; Deschutes Obsidian Stout; Dieu du Ciel Péché Mortel Imperial Coffee Stout; Grand Teton Brewing Black Cauldron Imperial Stout; Great Divide Brewing Yeti Imperial Stout; Napa Smith Bonfire Imperial Porter; North Coast Brewing Old Rasputin Russian Imperial Stout; Port Brewing Santa's Little Helper; Stone Brewing Imperial Russian Stout.

CHEESE AFFINITIES: This well-populated beer category embraces a broad style range that makes cheese recommendations especially challenging. Is the stout dry or syrupy sweet? Is it moderate in alcohol and medium bodied, or as viscous as maple syrup? Even mellow blue cheeses can vanquish some dry stouts, for example, while an Imperial stout, with its alcoholic power and residual sugar, doesn't bow to many blues. The stronger and sweeter the beer, the more robust the cheese can be.

In most cases, the malt-forward character of stout and porter complements cheeses with nutty or brown-butter aromas, and cheeses that leave a subtle sweet impression. The alpine wheels of France and Switzerland—such as Beaufort and Gruyère—come to mind on both counts. Buttery, relatively mild blue cheeses and creamy, mellow Cheddars can be good matches, but be wary of assertive blues with dry stouts and porters. Aged Goudas, with their candy-like butterscotch and salted-caramel flavors, need the heft of an Imperial stout or Imperial porter for balance. Triple-cream cheeses complement the texture of these smooth, silky brews and can be as pleasurable with a stout's mocha flavors as cream in coffee.

Mature **Comté,** aged for a year or more, has riveting depth of flavor. With profound aromas of roasted hazelnuts, sautéed onion, and bacon and a lingering aftertaste of butter and cream, it is a far more engaging cheese than the young supermarket Comté that many shoppers use for sandwiches. Produced from raw cow's milk in the Jura Mountains of eastern France, the hefty, 80-pound wheels of Comté may be sold as young as four months, but twelve to twenty-four months brings them to greatness. A deep-yellow to gold paste is one sign of a more mature cheese, but a big meaty fragrance and concentrated sweet flavor are the real giveaways. A nutty aged Comté heightens the roasted-grain character of stouts and porters and has enough intensity to partner the high-alcohol Imperial brews.

Young wheels of **Barely Buzzed,** a cow's milk Cheddar from Utah's Beehive Cheese Company, are rubbed with ground coffee and dried lavender and aged for about six months. This unusual rind treatment produces a subtle coffee scent throughout the mature cheese, mingled with aromas of Kahlúa, Mexican chocolate, and smoke. A stout or porter, with its own coffee notes, produces a lingering aroma echo, like having a double shot of espresso.

Ireland's **Cashel Blue,** an especially mellow and nutty blue-veined cow's milk cheese, melts in the mouth when ripe. Moist and spreadable, even creamy just under the rind, it moderates the bitter edge of a stout and makes the beer taste sweeter. Remove the cheese from the refrigerator a few hours before serving to bring it fully to room temperature and allow the buttery texture to show at its best.

MORE CHEESES TO TRY: With stout or porter: Beaufort; Berkswell; Bleu d'Auvergne; Brillat-Savarin; Challerhocker; Coolea; Cowgirl Creamery Mt. Tam; Ewephoria; Garrotxa; Gruyère; Hook's 5-Year Cheddar; Jean Grogne; Lamb Chopper; St. Agur; Vermont Butter & Cheese Cremont; Willamette Valley Farmstead Gouda. **With Imperial stout or Imperial porter:** Abbaye de Belloc; L'Amuse Gouda; Beecher's Flagship Reserve; Beemster XO; Challerhocker; Fourme d'Ambert; Stichelton; Stilton.

Top to bottom: Cashel Blue,
Barely Buzzed

STORMY WEATHER

FIRESTONE
VELVET MERLIN
OATMEAL STOUT

A dark and stormy night calls for a brooding, impenetrable brew like Velvet Merlin. Its creamy texture and aromas of coffee and caramel complement these dreamy dessert cheeses: the nutty, faintly sweet goat's-milk Garrotxa from Spain; the voluptuous double-cream Cremont from Vermont; and Spain's La Peral, a meaty and mellow cow's-milk blue.

**Top to bottom: La Peral,
Cremont, Garrotxa**

Top to bottom: Caveman Blue, Pecorino Ginepro, Délice de Bourgogne

TRIPEL (TRIPLE)

STYLE NOTES: The Trappist monks at Belgium's Westmalle Abbey brewery created a new category of beer in the 1950s when they christened their strongest pale ale a *tripel*. Some authorities say the word refers to the high quantity of malt used in the brew; others claim that it comes from a medieval practice of marking the casks of strong beers with three *X*'s. Whatever the term's origins, tripels persist as high-proof golden ales brewed largely with pale malts. Other Trappist abbeys and Belgian brewers produce tripels today, as do a few American craft breweries, but Westmalle's version is widely considered a benchmark.

The classic tripel is unfiltered, with a hazy golden to pale amber color. Poured into a chalice—the widemouthed stemmed glass that is a tripel's traditional serving vessel—it throws a dense, creamy, and enduring head. A lacy webbing of foam, known as Belgian lace, clings to the glass as the beer level diminishes. Fruity and spicy aromas (apricot, banana, burnt orange peel, gingerbread, spice cake) leap from the glass, thanks in part to high carbonation. Many tripels are bottle conditioned (refermented in the bottle), giving them a fine, Champagne-like mousse. They can be highly hopped, especially in American hands. A dry, hoppy, bitter finish is common, but some tripels leave a sweet impression from candi sugar added to the wort to boost the alcohol.

Stoutness is a given in tripels, which tend to fall within the range of 8 to 10 percent alcohol. Some brews show their strength with an almost whiskey-like flavor, while others mask it dangerously well. Tripels are not beers to drink with abandon, although you may want to.

BEERS TO TRY: Anderson Valley Brother David's Triple; Arend Tripel; Boulevard Long Strange Tripel; The Bruery Batch 300; Chimay Tripel (Chimay Blanche); De Dolle Dulle Teve; Malheur 10; Tripel Karmeliet; Westmalle Tripel.

CHEESE AFFINITIES: Potent tripels welcome cheeses with comparable strength of character. Delicate or mild-mannered cheeses tend to be outgunned by a tripel's power, although full-flavored triple-cream cheeses can hold their own. Seek out well-aged cheeses such as Cheddar and Dry Jack; nutty sheep's milk wheels such as Ossau-Iraty and Zamorano; and moderately pungent washed-rind cheeses. For tripels with a hint of sweetness, like Arend, try cheeses with whiskey and caramel notes, such as extra-aged Gouda, and buttery, mellow blue cheeses.

A triple-cream cheese from France's Burgundy region, **Délice de Bourgogne** tops the charts for richness. This luscious cow's milk cheese has a whipped-butter texture and a salty crème-fraîche tang that keeps it from being cloying. Spread the cheese on walnut bread and note how a tripel's bitter finish refreshes the palate between bites.

Rogue Creamery's **Caveman Blue** occupies the middle ground in the realm of blue-veined cheeses, with bold but not biting flavor and concentration without excess salt. A cow's milk wheel with a natural rind, Caveman has a seductive aroma of nuts and buttermilk that develops over six months in the aging cellar. The texture is dense, buttery, almost fudgy. It's particularly compatible with tripels that show some sweetness.

Pecorino Ginepro comes from northern Italy's Emilia-Romagna region, birthplace of balsamic vinegar. Perhaps inevitably, a local pecorino producer dreamed up a signature treatment for some wheels: repeated washings with balsamic vinegar and a coating of juniper berries (*ginepro* in Italian). After three to four months of aging, the 6-pound wheels are brushed clean and sold, their rinds dark and damp from the vinegar. Their firm, dryish ivory interiors smell like a broiled lamb chop, with lemony and grassy notes and a faint woodsy scent. Made from rich sheep's milk, Pecorino Ginepro leaves a lingering impression of sweetness and salt. Belgian-style tripel has the spice and strength of personality to match this fragrant, gamy cheese.

MORE CHEESES TO TRY: Abbaye de Belloc; Bleu des Basques; Bleu Mont Bandaged Cheddar; Cashel Blue; Chaumes; Chimay; Comté; Montgomery's Cheddar; MouCo ColoRouge; Ossau-Iraty; Petit Agour; Pierre Robert; Rocchetta (mixed-milk robiola); Tomme Brûlée; Vella Dry Monterery Jack.

WHEAT BEER, WITBIER, WEISSBIER, AND HEFEWEIZEN

STYLE NOTES: When the occasion calls for a thirst-quenching beverage, many beer lovers reach for a wheat beer. These popular pale brews have an easy quaffability thanks to their relatively low alcohol, brisk effervescence, and modest bitterness.

Many brewers make wheat beer—some year-round—and styles vary greatly. American, Belgian, and German approaches have some aspects in common, but noticeable differences, too.

Despite their name, wheat beers are rarely made entirely from wheat. More typically, wheat accounts for 30 to 50 percent of the grain base, with malted barley, and occasionally oats, making up the rest. High in protein, the wheat contributes a silky, viscous texture and an especially luxuriant head.

Most wheat beers have a pale straw to pale gold hue. Many are unfiltered, with a hazy or even cloudy aspect. Traditional recipes rely on pale malts—in some brews, the wheat isn't malted at all—so wheat beers don't offer much, if any, toast or toffee aroma. Brewers use a light hand with hops to keep from dominating the subtle malt, so most wheat beers aren't hugely aromatic. Their appeal lies in their drinkability and freshness, welcome qualities at a warm-weather lunch or at the start of a meal.

And now for the differences. The classic **Belgian witbier** (Flemish for "white beer") is brewed with spices and other fragrant additions, typically dried bitter-orange peel and coriander. The aroma from these seasonings is subdued but detectable, along with other fruity notes, a lemony tartness, and a faint honeyed scent. Some tasters discern a floury fragrance or the scent of cooked pasta, probably from the unmalted wheat used in the brew. Witbiers have a creamy mouthfeel; a fine, full effervescence; and a dry finish. Beers with *blanche* (French for "white") in the name are likely to be either witbiers from the French-speaking southern half of Belgium or Belgian-style witbiers from the New World.

German and German-style wheat beers have their own nomenclature. In the German tradition, the term *weissbier* ("white beer") or *hefeweizen* ("yeast wheat") indicates a brew made from at least 50 percent malted wheat. Unlike their Belgian counterparts, these beers aren't spiced. Their signature fragrance suggests banana, cloves, and yeast, reminiscent of a slice of warm banana bread. They have the cloudiness, prickly carbonation, and low bitterness of other wheat beers and no noticeable hops aroma. A few breweries make a *dunkelweizen* ("dark wheat" beer), using wheat plus darker malts. These pale amber beers have a more layered scent of banana, vanilla, and caramel and can have a slightly sour finish.

American wheat beers march to their own drummer, of course. They may or may not have Belgian-style spicing (check the label) or the banana and clove scent attributable to German yeasts. They may be cloudy or clear, but most examples will conform to the European model of pale color, modest alcohol, light hopping, and restrained bitterness.

BEERS TO TRY: Allagash White; Anchor Brewing Summer Beer; Ayinger Ur-Weisse; Blanche de Bruxelles; Franziskaner Hefe-Weisse; Hitachino Nest White Ale; Napa Smith Ginger Wheat Beer; New Belgium Sunshine Wheat; Ommegang Witte; Pyramid Hefeweizen; Schneider Wiesen Edel-Weisse; St. Bernardus Witbier; Widmer Brothers Hefeweizen.

CHEESE AFFINITIES: To match the understated personality of a wheat beer, look primarily to young, fresh cheeses with simple buttery or milky flavors. These soft, supple cheeses appreciate the firm carbonation of wheat beer, and they match the beer in modest flavor intensity. Context plays a role, too. On a balmy summer evening, a wheat beer suits the moment, especially with an appetizer of goat cheese and roasted beets or a feta-sprinkled Greek salad.

Burrata is mozzarella's richer and more fashionable relative, a southern Italian specialty now made in America. At a glance, it may look like a conventional ball of mozzarella, but burrata hides a secret. Slice into it to reveal the luscious filling, a mixture of mozzarella curds and heavy cream. Freshness is paramount; within a week, burrata can begin to sour. Well-made burrata has a thin skin and a creamy, buttery, sweet interior with just a hint of cultured-milk tang. Pair it with sliced tomatoes or roasted red peppers and a cold wheat beer.

Franklin Peluso, a third-generation California cheesemaker, produces the cheese his grandfather created, a 6-pound cow's milk square now known as **Franklin's Teleme.** Lightly dusted with rice flour, the floppy square stands about 2 inches tall and is ripened for only two weeks before release. At that youthful stage, it is soft, mild, and buttery, with a sour-cream fragrance. If allowed to mature for another three to four weeks, it becomes silky inside, even runny, with appetizing mushroom aromas. At any stage, it has a delicacy suited to wheat beer.

Laura Chenel Cabécou, from the California creamery that popularized goat cheese in the United States, is a fresh, rindless chèvre packed in olive oil with herbs and peppercorns. The little disks weigh only about 1½ ounces each, ideal for one person. Warming them in the oven until they quiver makes them irresistible. But even at room temperature, they have a pleasing creamy texture, herbaceous fragrance, and lively tang. Accompany with roasted peppers or roasted tomatoes, a crusty baguette, and wheat beer.

MORE CHEESES TO TRY: Asiago Fresco; Bellwether Farms Crescenza; Chaumes; feta; fresh goat cheese (no rind); Jasper Hill Farm Constant Bliss; mozzarella.

Top to bottom: Burrata,
Franklin's Teleme, Laura Chenel
Cabécou

Juniper Grove Dutchman's Flat

Fermented slowly at cool temperatures with yeasts that work on the bottom of the fermenting vat, lagers constitute the other main branch of the beer family.

They range from light, bright pilsners to robust doppelbocks, but what unites all lagers is *lagering,* or an extended chilling period before bottling. During this month or two of low-temperature storage, lagers become smoother and more mellow.

Although the word *lager* is often associated with watery, mass-market beers, some of the most acclaimed craft beers are lagers. Made with quality ingredients and care, lagers can be as engaging as any ale. Compared to ales, which owe a lot of their seductive aromas to warm fermentation and ale yeast, lagers are more buttoned-up. Crisp, direct, and uncomplicated, well-made lagers reward drinkers with a pure expression of hops and malt.

Top to bottom: Pleasant Ridge Reserve, Cameo

AMBER LAGER AND CALIFORNIA COMMON

STYLE NOTES: Malt makes the first impression in amber lager and California common, related styles with many similarities and a few key differences. In both color and aroma, these beers show the influence of caramel malts: a darker hue (typically amber to copper), fuller body, richer flavor, and toastier aroma than one finds in a pilsner or standard American lager.

Both of these styles hover around 5 percent alcohol, moderate enough for midday enjoyment. Any higher and they would be venturing into bock territory. Hops aroma may or may not be apparent; the most famous California common—Anchor Steam—shows some. Bitterness balances the malty sweetness and boosts the refreshment value, although neither style is ever aggressively bitter. Amber lagers typically tally below 30 IBUs; California commons can climb higher.

Other differences reflect the hybrid nature of California commons. Although made with lager yeast, these beers aren't strictly lagers. Custom calls for fermenting them at the warm temperatures used for ales, so the finished brew tends to have more of the fruity aromas that ale fermentations elicit.

This offbeat process emerged out of necessity, not by design. California common traces its origin to the Golden State's gold rush, when fortune-seekers came west in droves. These thirsty prospectors wanted to brew lager but lacked the necessary ice or refrigeration. So they improvised with lager yeasts and shallow fermenters to keep the wort cool. Their adaptations yielded what came to be known as steam beer—a highly effervescent brew that fused lager ingredients with ale technique. Some trace the origins of the name to the steam-whistle sound the kegs made when tapped. Others say these gold rush beers were fermented on cool San Francisco rooftops, and when the fog lifted in the morning, steam would rise.

Anchor Steam, still brewed in San Francisco, has preserved and popularized this style. Today, "steam" is a registered trademark of the Anchor Brewing Company, so other brews made in that fashion are marketed as California common.

BEERS TO TRY: Abita Amber; Anchor Steam; Brooklyn Lager; Flat Earth Brewing Element 115; Flying Dog Brewery Old Scratch Amber Lager; Samuel Adams Boston Lager; Steamworks Steam Engine Lager.

CHEESE AFFINITIES: These malt-forward beers appreciate cheeses with a hint of sweetness, although not the full-blown caramel flavor of, say, an aged Gouda. Asiago, Piave, and similar aged cow's milk cheeses come to mind. Moderate in alcohol, bitterness, and intensity, amber lager and California common pair better with mellow cheeses than with sharp, stinky, tangy, or otherwise extreme types.

Extra-Aged Asiago from Sartori, a Wisconsin producer, does not have the peppery bite you might expect in a year-old wheel of this type. Instead, the extra time in the cellar renders this cow's milk cheese more nutty and mellow. Straw to pale gold in color, with a Cheddar-like appearance, it feels crumbly on the tongue at first but dissolves to a creamy, almost buttery finish. The nuttiness reinforces the toasted-malt aroma of amber lager and California common; and the moderate flavor intensity of cheese and beer align.

A celebrity among American cheeses for its multiple "Best of Show" ribbons in competition, Wisconsin's **Pleasant Ridge Reserve** sets the standard for alpine-style cheeses in the United States. Initially modeled after France's Beaufort, this farmstead cheese from raw cow's milk has now established its own identity, characterized by profound aromas of roasted peanuts, caramel, and bacon. Produced only when the cows are on pasture, a fourteen-month-old wheel has a rich golden color and a lingering mellow, meaty, nutty flavor. A malty amber lager or California common amplifies its core of sweetness.

Redwood Hill Cameo, like its better-known sibling, Camellia, is a bloomy-rind California goat's milk cheese in the Camembert style. But Cameo is twice the size of Camellia—8 ounces versus 4—and ripens more reliably. When it gives to slight pressure, it is likely at its peak: silky and voluptuous inside, with mushroom aromas and a peppery fragrance imparted by the pink peppercorns that decorate the surface. Unlike many goat cheeses in this style, it is more nutty and sweet than tangy, a profile that complements the malty nature of an amber lager or California common.

MORE CHEESES TO TRY: Capriole Julianna; Fiscalini San Joaquin Gold; Garrotxa; Montasio; Montcabrer; Murcia al Vino (Drunken Goat); Piave; Juniper Grove Farm Tumalo Tomme.

Top to bottom: St. Agur,
Garrotxa, Abbaye de Belloc

BOCK AND DOPPELBOCK

STYLE NOTES: The richly malty bock and doppelbock styles originated in Germany centuries ago, and today's fans will find many examples in American brewpubs. Beer historians trace the name to Einbeck, a German brewing town that specialized in extra-strong lagers for export, and they theorize that *beck* evolved into *bock* over time.

Bock gave rise to *doppelbock* (double bock), a name that, like many aspects of beer culture, has an element of hyperbole. Dopplebocks are indeed stronger, maltier, and heavier than bocks, but nowhere near twice as strong. A traditional bock might fall in the 6 to 7 percent alcohol range, while a doppelbock is likely to tally between 7 and 10 percent.

Paulaner monks at a monastery near Munich brewed the original doppelbocks in the eighteenth century and referred to these dark, malty brews as "liquid bread." No doubt the beer was particularly appreciated during the fast days of Lent, when the monks were restricted to a liquid diet. Doppelbock versus water? No contest.

The famous Paulaner Salvator, although no longer associated with a monastery, is a descendant of the friars' brew. Many modern brewers honor this history by christening their doppelbocks with a name that ends in "-ator."

Bocks and doppelbocks are typically clear in aspect and range in color from amber to cola. Full-bodied and richly malty, with a smooth and satiny texture, these brews seduce with aromas of roasted grain, molasses, spice cake, grass, cooked wild rice, and wood smoke. Doppelbocks that incorporate deeply roasted chocolate malts may even smell like chocolate cake. Classic German examples have little or no hops aroma, but American brews may show the spicy fragrance of American hops. Bocks and doppelbocks are invariably malt-centric and often notably sweet, with just enough bitterness to balance the malt.

BEERS TO TRY: Anchor Brewing Anchor Bock; Ayinger Celebrator Doppelbock; Bell's Lager; Boulevard Boss Tom's Golden Bock; Grand Teton Double Vision Doppelbock; Paulaner Salvator; Samuel Adams Double Bock; Smuttynose S'Muttonator; Spaten Optimator; Sudwerk Doppel Bock; Weissenohe Bonator.

CHEESE AFFINITIES: With their robust, roasted-grain flavors, bocks and doppelbocks pair best with aged cheeses that have a similar core of sweetness. Nutty cow's-milk mountain cheeses like Beaufort and Appenzeller harmonize with these beers, as do mellow, buttery blue cheeses. Also consider Gouda and Gouda-style wheels, and sheep's milk cheeses with caramel and brown-butter notes, such as Abbaye de Belloc, as opposed to a sharper, more piquant sheep's milk cheese such as Roncal.

Aside from Roquefort, France's finest sheep's milk cheeses come from the Pyrenees Mountains, where sheep graze on flavorful high-altitude pasture in season. One standout among these Basque mountain wheels is **Abbaye de Belloc,** made at a Benedictine monastery from local milk. Weighing roughly 10 pounds, the wheels receive about six months of aging, rendering them dense, firm, and silky, especially when shaved with a cheese plane. The aroma fuses brown butter, nuts, and caramel, with little or none of the lanolin scent that pervades some sheep's milk cheeses. A bock or doppelbock finds an echo in Abbaye de Belloc's mellow nature and gentle brown-sugar sweetness.

Garrotxa, an aged goat's milk cheese from Spain, sports a thin rind coated in penicillium, the same mold that makes the veins in blue cheese. The ivory interior is dense, semifirm, and smooth, melting readily on the tongue. Nutty aromas give way to a faint caramel-like finish, a quality reminiscent of the goat's-milk caramel known as *cajeta* or *dulce de leche*. The rich, malty heart and evident sweetness in many bocks and doppelbocks match the cheese's subtle cooked-milk taste.

The French blue-veined **St. Agur** qualifies as a double-cream cheese, a designation that reflects its high fat content. Made with cream-enriched cow's milk, it has a moist, plush, dreamy texture that makes converts of even the most resolute blue-cheese resisters. Fans of piquant, spicy blue cheese: Look elsewhere. St. Agur is mild and buttery, a mellow complement to a velvety-smooth bock or doppelbock.

MORE CHEESES TO TRY: Bleu des Basques; Hoch Ybrig; Idiazábal; La Peral; Le Maréchal; Spring Brook Tarentaise; Tomme du Lévézou; Tumalo Farms Pondhopper; Vermont Shepherd Cheese; Wisconsin Sheep Dairy Dante.

MAIBOCK

STYLE NOTES: Brewers don't require much of an occasion to brew a special-occasion beer. The coming of spring is reason enough. March may be bitterly cold, but by May, the weather could be warm enough to sit outside with friends and a mug, and that's worth celebrating, no?

Such optimism possibly inspired the creation of *Maibock* ("May" beer), a lager that needs several weeks of cold storage to mellow before its spring release. Of German origin, the style has taken hold in America's brewpubs, where it often provides the excuse for a festival.

Typically a touch less malty and more bitter than traditional bock, Maibock tends to be a shade lighter, too. Most Maibocks are crystal clear and golden to amber in hue—hardly pale yet often classified as *helles bock* (pale bock) to distinguish them from the darker bocks and doppelbocks. Yet, like other bocks, they are relatively strong and richly malty, with an alcohol level that may top 7 percent. They have a sweet, toasty middle but a moderately dry to dry finish, with enough hops bitterness to make them refreshing in warm weather. Compared to most pilsners, the classic Maibock has more color, fuller body, and more alcoholic warmth.

Brewers consider Maibock a seasonal offering, for enjoyment from late spring through summer. Helles bocks, which some craft brewers identify as blonde lagers, are brewed year-round.

BEERS TO TRY: Einbecker Mai-Ur-Bock; Elysian Brewing Ambrosia Maibock; Gordon Biersch Blonde Bock; Gordon Biersch Maibock; Rogue Dead Guy Ale; Spaten Maibock.

CHEESE AFFINITIES: The malty depth and fullness of a Maibock complement cheeses with buttery and nutty scents. Consider alpine-style cow's milk cheeses like Beaufort, with their roasted-nut aromas and sweet finish. Aged sheep's milk cheeses with brown-butter aromas appreciate Maibock's malty personality, as do buttery triple-cream cheeses and bloomy-rind cheeses such as Brie. Tangy goat cheeses and Cheddars aren't as pleasing with Maibocks; these high-acid cheeses can make the beer seem too sweet.

Brie de Coulommiers—or Coulommiers, for short—belongs to the same bloomy-rind family as Brie de Meaux, the beloved French cow's milk cheese. But the latter can't be sold in the United States because it doesn't meet FDA aging requirements for raw-milk cheese. Fortunately, Coulommiers is a more than adequate stand-in. Made in a nearly identical manner but with pasteurized milk, Coulommiers satisfies import laws. It is smaller in diameter and thicker than Brie de Meaux, but the flavor profile is similar. When on the young side, Coulommiers has a snow-white rind and a buttery, sour cream–like flavor. With more maturity, the cheese develops some reddish markings on the rind; the interior becomes more supple and silky; and a savory aroma emerges, suggesting mushrooms and aged beef. Whether youthful or fully ripe, Coulommiers has the buttery, faintly nutty quality that responds to a beer on the malty side.

Not as common at American cheese counters as comparable cheeses like Beaufort and Comté, **Abondance** is worth seeking out. Made from raw cow's milk in the French Alps, the 15- to 30-pound wheels receive at least three months' aging but often twice that. More mature wheels have a firm, dense, smooth, and fine-grained texture; aromas of brown butter, light caramel, and grass; and a mellow, fruity finish. The extra alcohol in a Maibock gives the beer enough substance for this cheese's concentrated flavor.

Although many people purchase **Parmigiano Reggiano** only for cooking, it is one of the world's great table cheeses. To preserve its granular texture, break it into rocky chunks with a short, triangular-bladed Parmesan knife; don't try to slice it. The giant wheels receive a minimum of one year of aging, but a two-year-old Parmigiano Reggiano will be even better, with a deep gold color; a pleasing crunch from protein crystals; and a toasty, nutty, brown-butter aroma with a hint of orange peel. At its best, Parmigiano Reggiano will be complex, elegant, and mellow, perfectly balanced between sweetness, acidity, and salt. Its concentration and robust, nutty aroma call for strong, malty beers like Maibock.

MORE CHEESES TO TRY: Beaufort; Camembert; Comté; Emmental; Fiore Sardo; Garrotxa; Gruyère; Rouge et Noir Triple Crème Brie; Seal Bay Triple Cream Brie.

Top to bottom: Abondance, Parmigiano
Reggiano, Brie de Coulommiers

AMERICAN CHEDDAR SMACKDOWN

MENDOCINO BREWING COMPANY
RED TAIL ALE

Comparing three fine Cheddars from California (Fiscalini), Wisconsin (Bleu Mont), and Vermont (Cabot Clothbound) will help you assess the domestic state of the art. For a ringer, throw in Keen's, Quickes, or Montgomery's Cheddar from England, widely considered that country's best. With its balance of toasty malt and floral hops, Red Tail Ale can manage any Cheddar in its path, from mellow to tangy.

Fiscalini

Bleu Mont

Cabot

Top to bottom: Fiscalini Bandaged Cheddar, Bleu Mont Bandaged Cheddar, Cabot Clothbound Cheddar

Top to bottom: Leiden, Dante

MÄRZEN AND OKTOBERFEST

STYLE NOTES: In the days before refrigeration, Bavarian brewers depended on cold weather and natural ice to keep fermentations and finished brews cool. Brewing followed more seasonal rhythms then, often ceasing during the summer months, when beer so easily spoiled. Typically, the last lager of the spring season would be brewed in March and stored in cool natural caves or underground cellars over the summer. With care and luck, the March beer—or *Märzenbier*—would still be in good shape and in good supply for autumn harvest celebrations. By the late nineteenth century, malty Märzen-style beer had come to symbolize Oktoberfest, Munich's world-renowned outdoor fair.

In Germany today, only a handful of Munich breweries have the legal right to brew *Oktoberfestbier* and supply the festival. American craft brewers can ignore German law, of course, and many produce a seasonal Oktoberfest, among the most popular of brewpub styles.

To most consumers, little differentiates an Oktoberfest from its predecessor, Märzen, which some brewers make and bottle year-round. Both are medium-bodied, malt-focused beers with low-level bitterness and little hop aroma. Oktoberfest brews tend to be golden in hue, with Märzens mostly darker, leaning toward amber or auburn. Both open with malty sweetness—more toasted bread than caramel—but finish dry. Both are moderately effervescent, sometimes creamy but never cloying.

Topping out at around 6 percent alcohol, Oktoberfest and Märzen steer clear of pretention. These are easy-drinking stein beers, not offended by a thick glass mug.

BEERS TO TRY: Ayinger Oktoberfest; Boulevard Brewing Bob's '47 Oktoberfest; Gordon Biersch Märzen; Grand Teton Fest Bier Märzen Lager; Heavy Seas Märzen; Paulaner Oktoberfest Märzen; Samuel Adams Oktoberfest; Sudwerk Märzen .

CHEESE AFFINITIES: The malty nature of Märzen and Oktoberfest makes the case for aged cheese, the kind with the toasted-nut, brown-butter, or caramel aromas that malt complements. Consider mature sheep's milk wheels in the style of Manchego or Abbaye de Belloc; nutty alpine-style cheeses similar to Comté; Cheddars that are more mellow than tangy; and Gouda-like cheeses made with any type of milk.

Cabot Clothbound Cheddar originated from an unlikely collaboration between Vermont's largest cheese producer (Cabot Creamery, a fourteen-hundred-member cooperative) and one of its smallest, Jasper Hill Farm. Cabot's crew had plenty of experience making rindless block Cheddar in sealed plastic bags but little expertise in traditional English-style wheels, which mature in contact with air. So they turned to neighboring Jasper Hill, whose proprietors have developed a specialty in *affinage,* or cheese maturation. Cabot starts the cheese-making process, producing 35-pound wheels from pasteurized cow's milk from a single farm. But when the cheeses are less than a week old, they move to the underground cellars at Jasper Hill. They remain there for about a year, time enough for a rind to develop and for flavor to bloom. A mature Cabot Clothbound Cheddar offers aromas of freshly mown grass, toasted nuts, toffee, and candle wax. Less tangy than English Cheddars, with little or no acid bite, it has a gentle sweetness that responds to a malt-forward Märzen.

Dutch **Leiden** bears a strong resemblance to Gouda, Holland's best-known cheese. Leiden (or Leyden) is slightly lower in fat but made in the same shape and by a similar method. But whereas some Gouda has spices added, Leiden always does. Whole cumin seeds fleck its pale gold interior, infusing the smooth, semisoft to semifirm paste with a warm, spicy scent. Leiden's mellow flavor results from a technique called curd washing. Rinsing the fresh curds with water yields a "sweeter" cheese in the end, with lower acidity and little or no tang. A wedge of Leiden makes a satisfying lunch with whole-grain bread, sliced sweet onions, and mustard—and a mug of Märzen or Oktoberfest beer to complete the picture.

A creation of the Wisconsin Sheep Dairy Cooperative, **Dante** is a seasonal cheese, made only between February and September and aged for about six months. A mature ten-pound wheel has a firm, dry, golden interior—darker than most comparable sheep's milk cheeses—with abundant aromas of toasted nuts and brown butter and a sweetness that lingers. A malt-forward brew like a Märzen or Oktoberfest hits a lot of the same flavor notes.

MORE CHEESES TO TRY: Abbaye de Belloc; Abondance; Barinaga Ranch Baserri; Beehive Cheese Barely Buzzed; Garrotxa; Jura du Montagne; Midnight Moon; Parmigiano Reggiano; Pleasant Ridge Reserve; Stilton; Tumalo Farms Fenacho; Vermont Shepherd Cheese; Zamorano.

PILSNER

STYLE NOTES: With its modest alcohol content and crisp, uncomplicated flavor, a cold pilsner has thirst-slaking appeal on a warm day. The traditional pilsner vessel—a tall, slender glass with a narrow base and wider rim—shows this brew to perfection, encouraging a thick, lofty head and showcasing the beer's gleaming yellow-gold clarity. No wonder the world's first pilsner seduced consumers immediately. Introduced in Bohemia in 1842, about the same time that mass-produced glasses began to replace clunky tankards, the eye-catching pilsner delighted drinkers accustomed to darker and cloudier brews.

Pilsner (or pilsener) takes its name from the Bohemian town of Plzen (or Pilsen), now part of the Czech Republic. That's where the style originated, in a brand-new brewery that still produces the famed *Pilsner Urquell* ("original pilsner") today.

An authentic pilsner owes its bright straw color to the use of lightly kilned malts, a departure from the dark Munich malts commonplace when pilsner debuted. These pale malts typically contribute some bread-dough aromas and a gentle honeyed sweetness, but you won't find roasted, toasty, or caramel aromas—the signature of darker malts—in a pilsner. The classic pilsner hop is Saaz, a variety that thrives in the Czech Republic and contributes a fresh, delicate aroma and low-level bitterness. Pilsners are easy-drinking, effervescent beers that don't linger on the palate and don't demand a lot of attention.

Czech, German, and Belgian pilsners exhibit some subtle differences. Czech brews tend to be a little darker, German more bitter, and Belgian sweeter. American craft brewers, with no tradition to bind them, feel free to interpret the pilsner style as they like. Some are even making an "Imperial pilsner," with elevated alcohol. Mass-market American pilsners, which often include adjunct grains such as corn or rice, have little to offer beyond fizz and rarely merit the calories.

BEERS TO TRY: Great Divide Nomad; Lagunitas Pils; Moonlight Brewing Reality Czech; Oskar Blues Mama's Little Yella Pils; Pinkus Müller Brewery Pinkus Pils; Trumer Pils; Victory Prima Pils.

CHEESE AFFINITIES: The low-key personality of pilsner calls for cheeses with similar restraint. Fresh and lightly ripened cheeses, like young robiolas and chèvres, are a good bet, as their delicate aromatics suit these light-bodied beers. Bold cheeses might mask a pilsner's subtlety, and the undemanding nature of pilsner gives simple, fresh cheeses a chance to shine. Surprisingly, some well-aged cheeses with a subtle sweet finish—like Fiscalini San Joaquin Gold, Capriole's Julianna, and the goat's milk Montcabrer—can also work with pilsner, highlighting the beer's malty nature.

The vigorous carbonation in pilsner welcomes the contrast of a luscious triple-cream cheese such as **Brillat-Savarin.** This young French bloomy-rind cheese has the tongue-coating texture of whipped butter, and the pilsner's bubbles provide palate refreshment. It's as if they scrub away the fat, leaving you ready for the next bite. The ultra-smooth Brillat-Savarin is made from cow's milk enriched with crème fraîche, giving it a fluffy mouthfeel and delicate sour-cream tang. The velvety rind should be mostly white. A heavily mottled rind or shrunken appearance would indicate an overripe cheese that would likely smell and taste ammoniated. Try to buy from a merchant who cuts this cheese to order. Brillat-Savarin declines quickly in plastic wrap.

Mozzarella di bufala (buffalo-milk mozzarella) provides the foundation for the beloved *insalata caprese,* the salad that sends mozzarella sales soaring in summer. Sliced and layered with ripe tomatoes and basil, then drizzled with extra-virgin olive oil (no vinegar, please), *mozzarella di bufala* has a sweet, milky, uncomplicated taste and a moist, creamy texture. Enjoyed outdoors on a warm day, the salad needs only a cold pilsner to complete the picture of *la dolce vita.* A brew with more robust malt or hops would overpower this delicate cheese, ideally served before it's a week old.

Julianna, an aged raw-milk goat cheese from Indiana's Capriole farmstead creamery, is a petite, pretty 1-pound round cloaked with dried herbs. Its ivory interior is dense and moist, on the cusp between semisoft and semifirm, with an appealing creaminess and a gentle, mellow, non-tangy finish. The fragrance of lavender and rosemary permeates the interior but doesn't overwhelm it. Resembling a goat's milk version of the Corsican sheep's milk Brin d'Amour, Julianna has a subtle cooked-milk sweetness that blends easily with the grainy notes of a malty pilsner like Lagunitas Pils. Hoppy pilsners, such as Victory Prima Pils, don't match it as well.

MORE CHEESES TO TRY: Asiago Pressato; Beehive Cheese Promontory; Bosina; Brebiou; Cowgirl Creamery Mt. Tam; Fiscalini San Joaquin Gold; Franklin's Teleme; Fromage de Meaux; Harley Farms Monet; Montcabrer; mozzarella; Picandine.

Brillat-Savarin

DOG DAY LUNCH

**VICTORY
PRIMA PILS**

When it's too hot to cook, make a lunch from cheese and salad. Fresh, young cheeses with simple flavors have the most appeal in warm weather, and a crisp pilsner provides the refreshment. Add sliced tomatoes, cucumbers, ripe olives, sturdy bread. Lunch is served.

Top to bottom: Asiago Pressato, Harley Farms Monet, Bellwether Farms Sheep's Milk Ricotta

WHICH BEER WITH THAT CHEESE?

You've bought the cheese. Now choose the beer. Use this chart to steer yourself to a compatible match.

CHEESE	EXAMPLES	TRY
With fresh unripened or lightly ripened cheese	burrata, Crescenza, fresh chèvre, fromage blanc, mozzarella, ricotta, Stracchino, Teleme	kölsch or blonde ale, pilsner, wheat beer
With bloomy-rind cow's milk cheese	Brie, Camembert, Jasper Hill Constant Bliss, Mt. Townsend Seastack, Sweet Grass Dairy Green Hill	American pale ale, Belgian-style pale ale, bière de Champagne, bière de garde, Maibock, porter, saison, sour ale, stout
With bloomy-rind goat's milk cheese	Bucherondin, Cypress Grove Humboldt Fog, Monte Enebro, Redwood Hill Camellia and Cameo, Vermont Butter & Cheese Bijou and Coupole	American pale ale, IPA
With triple-cream cheese	Brillat-Savarin, Cowgirl Creamery Mt. Tam, Délice de Bourgogne, Nancy's Hudson Valley Camembert, Nettle Meadow Kunik, Pierre Robert, Rouge et Noir Triple Crème Brie, Seal Bay Triple Cream Brie	Belgian-style strong golden ale, pilsner, sour ale, tripel
With aged goat's milk cheese	Capriole Julianna, Garrotxa, Juniper Grove Tumalo Tomme, Patacabra, Tumalo Farms Pondhopper	American pale ale, bock or doppelbock, brown ale, IPA, Maibock, Märzen or Oktoberfest, porter

CHEESE	EXAMPLES	TRY
With alpine-style cow's milk cheese	Appenzeller, Beaufort, Comté, Fontina Val d'Aosta, Gruyère, Pleasant Ridge Reserve, Spring Brook Farm Tarentaise, Tête de Moine	amber lager or California common, Belgian-style strong golden ale, bière de garde, bock or doppelbock, brown ale, dubbel, porter, saison, stout or Imperial stout
With hard aged cow's milk cheese	Asiago, Caerphilly, Parmigiano Reggiano, Piave, Vella Dry Jack	amber lager or California common, bière de garde, bitter or ESB, saison
With aged sheep's milk cheese	Abbaye de Belloc, Carr Valley Marisa, Manchego, Ombra, Pecorino Toscano, Roncal, Vermont Shepherd, Zamorano	amber or red ale, brown ale, holiday ale, Märzen or Oktoberfest, tripel
With washed-rind cheese	Chimay, Cowgirl Creamery Red Hawk, Crave Brothers Les Frères, Durrus, Epoisses, Livarot, MouCo ColoRouge, Munster, Widmer Brick, Jasper Hill Farm Winnimere	barley wine, Belgian-style pale ale, Belgian-style strong golden ale, dubbel, tripel
With Cheddar and Cheddar-style cheese	Beecher's Flagship Reserve, Beehive Promontory, Cabot Clothbound Cheddar, Fiscalini Cheddar, Hook's Cheddar, Keen's Cheddar, Montgomery's Cheddar	amber or red ale, American pale ale, barley wine, bitter or ESB, IPA, Märzen or Oktoberfest, porter, sour ale, stout
With Gouda and Gouda-style cheese	L'Amuse Gouda, Beemster XO, Boerenkaas, Leiden, Marieke Gouda, Mimolette, Tumalo Farms Classico	amber ale, bière de Champagne, brown ale, dubbel, holiday ale, Märzen or Oktoberfest, porter, quadrupel, stout
With blue cheese (mellow and buttery)	Bleu d'Auvergne, Cashel Blue, Fourme d'Ambert, Jasper Hill Bayley Hazen Blue, Shropshire Blue, Stichelton, Stilton	barley wine, doppelbock, dubbel, Maibock, porter, stout or Imperial stout, quadrupel
With blue cheese (piquant and spicy)	Great Hill Blue, Rogue Caveman Blue, Rogue River Blue, Shepherd's Way Big Woods Blue, Valdeón	barley wine, dubbel, holiday ale, Imperial stout, quadrupel

GLOSSARY

ALE: One of two primary beer categories (the other being lager). Ale is the result when wort is fermented with so-called ale yeast *(Saccharomyces cerevisiae)*. This type of yeast prefers relatively warm fermentation temperatures and works rapidly on the top of the fermenting vat. Largely due to the influence of the yeast, ales tend to be fruitier, spicier, and more aromatically complex than lagers.

CANDI SUGAR: Caramelized sugar that brewers sometimes use to boost the alcohol content of beer without adding body. Relying on malt sugar alone to achieve the desired alcohol would yield a heavier-bodied beer. The use of candi sugar—usually in liquid form—is common for many Belgian and Belgian-style ales, such as dubbels and tripels.

CRAFT BEER: The Brewers Association (BA) defines craft brewers as "small, independent, and traditional." To the BA, *small* means an annual output of six million barrels of beer or less. *Independent* means that the brewery is not controlled by a larger, non-craft brewer. And, to simplify slightly, *traditional* indicates that the brewery's flagship brew or the majority of its production is all-malt beer. In this context, *malt* means malted barley, and the intent is to exclude brewers who use cheaper grains like corn and rice to lighten flavor.

IBU: International Bitterness Units, the standard measure of bitterness in beer. IBU values are determined scientifically by measuring iso-alpha acids—the source of bitterness—in finished beer. In theory, IBU values range from 1 to about 100, although few beers measure below 8 or 10 and some extreme brews—such as some double IPAs and barley wines—can reach 120 IBUs.

LAGER: One of two primary beer categories (the other being ale). Lager is the result when wort is fermented with so-called lager yeast *(Saccharomyces pastorianus)*. This type of yeast prefers relatively cool fermentation temperatures and works slowly on the bottom of the fermenting vat. Lagers tend to be crisper, simpler, and less diverse in flavor than ales. Another key difference: Lagers are *lagered,* or stored in cold conditions, for weeks or months before release to allow their flavor to mellow.

SESSION BEER: A brew of relatively low alcohol—typically, 5 percent alcohol or less—that won't inebriate the person who consumes a pint or three over a long session at the pub among friends.

WORT: The sweet liquid that brewers ferment into beer. Wort is extracted from grains (primarily barley but also wheat, rye, and oats) by first sprouting the grains, then kilning (roasting) them, crushing them, and boiling them in water. The wort is the fermentable liquid drawn off of this mash.

BIBLIOGRAPHY

Bamforth, Charles. *Beer: Tap into the Art and Science of Brewing.* New York: Oxford University Press, 2009.

BJCP Style Guidelines for Beer, Mead, and Cider: 2008 Edition. www.bjcp.org/docs/2008_stylebook.pdf.

Campbell, Seamus, and Robin Goldstein. *The Beer Trials.* New York: Fearless Critic Media, 2010.

Jackson, Michael, ed. *Beer.* New York, DK Publishing, 2007.

Mosher, Randy. *Tasting Beer: An Insider's Guide to the World's Greatest Drink.* North Adams, Mass.: Storey Publishing, 2009.

Oliver, Garrett. *The Brewmaster's Table.* New York: Harper Collins, 2003.

Oliver, Garrett, ed. *The Oxford Companion to Beer.* New York: Oxford University Press, 2012.

Saunders, Lucy. *The Best of American Beer & Food: Pairing and Cooking with Craft Beer.* Boulder: Brewers Publications, 2007.

ACKNOWLEDGMENTS

I am indebted to many people for assistance with this book. First and foremost, Adam Dulye helped me understand and categorize the chaotic world of craft beer. As chef and partner at two top San Francisco gastropubs (Monk's Kettle and Abbot's Cellar), Adam has an encyclopedic knowledge of the world's great beers, and he generously attempted to share some of his expertise with me. He introduced me to many of the most acclaimed cult brews, answered countless queries, and reviewed the completed manuscript. I can't thank Adam and the staff at Monk's Kettle enough. I'm also grateful to all of my Napa Valley cheese merchants for accommodating many special requests, but especially to Lassa Skinner, Ricardo Huijón, and the staff at Oxbow Cheese Merchant; James Ayers at Sunshine Foods; Annie Smith and her staff at Whole Foods Napa; and the ever-helpful crew at Tomales Bay Foods. I thank beer enthusiast Marty Pulvers for his encouragement and careful review of the manuscript and Eric Lafranchi of Taps Restaurant & Tasting Room in Petaluma, California, for allowing us to photograph in his busy pub. Photographer/designer Ed Anderson and prop stylist Carol Hacker, with her assistant Sherry Olsen, gave this book just the look I wanted, with a big assist from designers Tim Lynch and Diane Marsh. My tireless agent Carole Bidnick—trusted advisor, cheerleader, nudge, and friend—made sure my book proposal landed in the right place. My husband, Douglas Fletcher, has joined me on this beer journey with an enthusiasm that matches my own. And of course I am most grateful to Andrews McMeel editor Jean Lucas and publisher Kirsty Melville for embracing my idea and making the publishing process a collaboration and a pleasure.

BEER INDEX

CHEESE INDEX

CKER TSC

N SPRINGS E

AGASH WHI

KEASY   PIE

KAN · PERS